SAMMY

The Sporting Life of
S.M.J. WOODS

CLIFFORD JIGGENS

Sansom &
Company

First published in 1997 by
SANSOM & COMPANY
Bristol

© C. Jiggens

ISBN 1 900178 85 0

British Cataloguing-in-Publication Data.
A catalogue record for this book is available
from the British Library.

Typeset by Mayhew Typesetting, Rhayader, Powys
Printed in Great Britain by Bookcraft, Midsomer Norton

CONTENTS

Illustrations appear between
pages 64–65 and 96–97

To Beryl

Preface

Sammy Woods was one of the most popular of all players in the
Golden Age of cricket. A roar from the crowd usually greeted
him when he bustled out to the wicket, swinging his bat;
although it was as a bowler that he more often won matches. Above
all he was a 'character'. Indeed E.H.D. Sewell, who played for Essex
in Edwardian days and became a leading cricket writer between the
wars, declared that Sammy was *the* greatest character the game had
known.

Books about the cricket and cricketers of his time usually include
one or two of the countless stories about Sammy: well-remembered
anecdotes about that breakfast of hot lobsters washed down with ale
before claiming all ten wickets in an innings; or how, captaining the
Gentlemen, he hurriedly started an extra over after time and gave the
Players victory. It has often been difficult, sometimes impossible, to
decide which stories are apocryphal. Some of the most unlikely, in
fact, proved to be true.

Surprisingly there has never been a book devoted to Sammy,
excepting his own reminiscences. David Frith, in *The Fast Men*, said
that Sammy deserved a book to himself. Here it is: mainly about his
cricket and other sport but also a portrait, warts and all, of a colourful
personality and his freewheeling life style in those golden days (for
some) of Victoria and Edward.

My Reminiscences, published a few years before Sammy died, provided
only a starting point for research, for they are very sketchy
reminiscences, sometimes tantalisingly brief (even omitting altogether
mention of some notable feats and incidents), sometimes repetitive,
and not always accurate. From then it has been a long journey through
the recorded memories of his contemporaries – Grace, Jessop, Ranji,
Warner, and many more; *Wisden* and other year books; the files of
Cricket, Athletic News, and other sporting periodicals of the day; college
magazines; and many newspapers, especially county and local papers.

The author's thanks go to the many correspondents who have
helped with his queries, and to two or three elderly gentlemen who

knew Sammy and whose memories of him in his later years are quoted. The archives of Somerset Cricket Museum have proved fruitful, and librarians at Taunton, Bridgwater, Bristol, Brighton, and Tunbridge Wells, and at the British Newspaper Library, have been very helpful, too.

To mention just one name: special thanks to John Sarbutt, of Kiama, New South Wales, a distant relative of Sammy, who generously provided much family and other information.

The illustrations are from the author's own collection and the Somerset Cricket Museum archive. The author also gratefully acknowledges help given by South West Counties Newspapers Ltd, Taunton, in copying old photographs.

Colonial Boy

W.G. Grace called him 'a giant in size, in strength, and in pluck'. He was a natural athlete and games player who excelled at half a dozen sports: perhaps the finest all-round sportsman to have come out of Australia. He played cricket for both his native land and his adopted home of England, and at rugby he captained England in some memorable victories. On the cricket field he was one of the most feared fast bowlers of his day, an aggressive batsman, and an inspiring captain. His seemingly inexhaustible energy, his bravery, sportsmanship and generosity were legendary, and earned him the sobriquet 'Greatheart'.

Something of a Peter Pan character, he was a big man-boy whose enthusiasm for sport remained at schoolboy pitch. He never knew when he was beaten and abhorred a drawn game ('draws are no use – except for bathing' was a favourite saying). He would rather lose gloriously than struggle to an inconclusive end to a match.

Samuel Moses James Woods had a zest for life that comes to few. He was a rumbustious, gregarious character whose exploits off as well as on the field would have made him a favourite with the tabloid newspapers had he been around today; while his freely expressed views would have earned him a regular column. After Grace he was one of the first favourites of the cartoonists.

He was a great raconteur (and a fine singer, too), and for every tale he could tell there was one waiting to be told about him. He had his rough edges – very rough, sometimes – but his sporting prowess and cheery nature broke down social barriers in the class-ridden England of late Victorian and Edwardian years.

Although he spent his boyhood in Australia, and later saw much of the world on cricket tours and other travels, it was Somerset he loved and regarded as home. In return the people of the Western county took him to their hearts. Over the years their folk hero gradually acquired the local mannerisms of speech. So much at home did he seem that one might have thought that his family had originated in the Westcountry and that he had returned to his roots.

But it was not from Somerset or neighbouring counties, nor even from another part of England, that the Woods had come. Their homeland was across the Irish Sea.

Sammy's parents, John Woods and Margaret Ewing, were married in the Presbyterian meeting house at Ballylinney, county Antrim, in 1853. John, son of a farmer, had been born near Castleblayney, beside lake Muckno, in county Monaghan, almost midway between Dublin and Belfast. Margaret, who came from Ballyclare, also in county Antrim, was a blacksmith's daughter. John's occupation was given on his marriage certificate as labourer. In fact he worked on his father's farm, after having had a rudimentary education at a small school nearby. As well as being a farmer, his father, Moses, was an officer in the local yeomanry.

In 1845 disaster had come to Ireland when the potato crop failed, and in the next few years over a million people died of starvation or disease. Even more fled across the seas, the great majority to North America and most of the rest to other parts of Britain. Thousands of others decided to undertake the much longer and hazardous journey to Australia.

The famine was over by time the young couple (John was 25, his bride 18) married, but the exodus from Ireland still went on. John's imagination had been fired by a Belfast newspaper report of a lecture on New South Wales, and he determined to seek his fortune there. The wedding in May was quickly followed by farewells to family and friends as John and Margaret set sail in an emigrant ship, the *Talavera*, from Dublin. They landed in Sydney in September after a seemingly endless voyage.

John Woods had taken with him enough money to make a start. His main assets, however, were a determined spirit and enterprise. He immediately started work as a carrier and contractor, this at a time when Sydney, with a population of about 60,000, was growing fast. His first contract, to transport materials for the Parramatta railway, proved very profitable. With his own hands John placed on one of his drays at the Sydney wharves the first rail to be landed in New South Wales.

His next important contract was to take across the sandhills to Botany all the huge pipes for the Sydney waterworks, and this, too, was profitable. More big contracts followed, and although he met reverses, John prospered. He became the part-owner of a paper mill and invested in land. After having served as mayor of Sydney he declined a second term and instead took a leading role in starting the

Sydney Omnibus Company and became a director of several other enterprises.

In a volume, *Australian Men of Mark*, it was recorded: 'Never has he permitted himself to be beaten down by reverses, but he has ever shown himself to be possessed of indomitable perseverance, pluck, and determination' – qualities to be shown by one of his sons on the cricket grounds of the world. 'Brave in the storm' is the family motto.

While John Woods was building up his enterprises and serving in public life, his young wife was no less occupied in providing him with a large family. She had 13 children, all but two of whom survived their early days. The eighth child, and the third of the five boys, was Samuel Moses James, taking his second name from his farmer-grandfather back in Ireland.

Samuel – usually Sammy, sometimes Sam – was born on April 13, 1867, at Ashfield, Sydney. (The date and place are often wrongly stated, the latter usually as Glenfield, where the Woods family lived for a time) When the birth was registered, the occupation of the father, the 'labourer' of 14 years earlier, was given as 'gentleman'.

From now on the family home was to be in the northern harbour-side suburb of Manly, which boasts one of Sydney's finest ocean beaches. John Woods had decided to move there when he was about 40, around the time Sammy was born. His years of hard work were beginning to affect his health, and a doctor had advised fresh sea air. He was, in fact, one of the pioneers of the village, as Manly is still called: a one-time fishing hamlet that has grown into a popular seaside resort.

John was among the early residents who planted the pine trees on the Ocean Beach Reserve, one of the features of Manly. Although now a wealthy man, he was not one to sit back. The speculative nature of his mind led him to purchase land and property there and at the same time to create a steamship company which greatly improved the meagre communications between Manly and the city. He saw property values soar as a result of the steamer venture.

Sammy went to Royston College and Sydney Grammar School, which from Manly meant a trip of five or six miles by steamer, morning and evening. It was sometimes a rough journey in the ocean swell.

All the five Woods boys were athletes. The oldest, Harry, was to hold Australian records for running and jumping; and the second oldest, John, who was known as 'Stringy Bark', was reckoned by

Sammy to be one of the fastest bowlers he ever saw, though unfortunately rather erratic.

When 'Stringy Bark' bowled to some of Archie MacLaren's England team before the first Test match in Sydney on the 1901–2 tour (probably at Sammy's suggestion), he caused them not a little apprehension. One of his fast deliveries went full pitch just past MacLaren's head. Another cracked a post in an adjoining net, causing the batsman there to retire until danger was past. Before the Test, 'Stringy Bark' said to Sammy: 'Well I'm blowed. They are a lot of funks and I have backed them to win for £50.' As it happened England won by an innings (MacLaren scoring a century), whereupon 'Stringy' claimed to have bowled them into form. However they lost the remaining four Tests, enabling him to declare: 'I told you. They don't know the first bloody thing about fast bowling.'

Young Sammy soon developed a passion for cricket. He had first played with 'an odd piece of wood' as a bat in a scratch game 'in the outback'. In middle age he wrote some random reminiscences and recalled his schooldays:

> I fancy I was much keener on cricket than my brothers, as I know they wouldn't practise before breakfast and I did. On one occasion I played for the 2nd XI at ten o'clock, got my first 100 at Double Bay (Sydney), kept wicket and saw my first leg-break bowler and did the hat-trick for him, two ridiculous stumps and a catch. In the afternoon I played for the 1st XI v Sydney Grammar School. I fancy I got 10 and took 6–18.

Although he scored a century or two in these early days – an unbeaten 117 at the age of 13 was probably his first – he was regarded mainly as a bowler who was also (as he put it) 'a very steady and slow' batsman.

His most remarkable feat at the college was to take seven wickets in seven balls, and in one season he claimed 70 victims at an average cost of five runs. The proudest moment of his schooldays came, however, when he was only 10 and was awarded his first 'cap'. Sammy recalled the occasion long afterwards to fellow members of Somerset county cricket club.

An older brother (it must have been 'Stringy Bark') was captain of a boys' XI, all under 16. They were one short, so to his great delight and in spite of his young age Sammy was enlisted. He was the only one in knickerbockers, he remembered, and as the team's colour was light blue he borrowed a riband from a sister and wore it round his waist. 'Little did I fancy,' he said, 'that in the future I was to wear that same colour, which I love so well: that of Cambridge.'

Sammy scored five or six runs in each innings and took three wickets, and was highly praised by his brother for two 'good catches'. 'Stringy Bark' then presented a cap which Sammy, in a sentimental moment perhaps, was to say he prized even more than his Cambridge, Somerset, and international caps.

He remembered for a different reason another match his brother pressed him into joining. As a cricketer Sammy was to set several records, some of which still stand, and the most unusual was three ducks in this boyhood match. For some reason there was a third innings, and the youngster failed to score in each. Moreover the single over he bowled (of seven balls) was hit for 25 by a boy named Harry Donnan, later to play for Australia and earn a reputation as a stonewaller. However there was some excuse for Sammy's below-par performance this time. He had just spent several weeks laid up with an injury to his knee cap, which he had badly cut with a glass bottle.

At Christmas time the Woods boys usually went to the South Sea islands in a schooner. Sammy recalled:

> On one occasion we went to Levuka (Fiji) and were asked to play cricket for the whites against the natives. The natives won the toss, and when I left after the first day's play the score, as far as I remember, was 175 for 72. I know I accounted for 25 of them. I think some had come in twice, but they were so alike one couldn't tell t'other from which. They were not all out then, and as I had to leave next morning and didn't get an innings I don't know which side won.

It was a favourite story with Sammy; often recounted, the figures doubtless varying. A history of Fijian cricket shows, though, that the number of players fits in with the pattern of 'communal participation' in the game at that time.

On the way home the party called at another island and, confessed Sammy, 'I stole a stone god'. He still had it over 40 years later. 'The natives discovered their loss and came after us in canoes. Luckily a good breeze was blowing and we got out of reach of their arrows. I never went there again.'

Apart from cricket and rugby, boxing was a sport which attracted the youngster. One day on the steamer between Manly and Sydney the Woods boys made the acquaintance of a young black man named Peter Jackson, a deckhand. On the journey home after school the boys would box with Jackson, who knelt on one knee. One of Sammy's brothers mentioned him to their boxing instructor, Larry Foley, who after seeing Jackson declared: 'I will make him champion of Australia in a year.'

Jackson, who soon took that title, was a West Indian who adopted Australia as his home. But for his colour he might have become the world heavyweight champion. As it was, John L. Sullivan, the American champion, declined to fight a black man. However, Gentleman Jim Corbett took Jackson on for a $10,000 purse in San Francisco, a fight which was stopped after 61 rounds, lasting four hours, and declared a draw. Years after his own sparring with Jackson on the boat, Sammy was to sit at the ringside in London and see him knock out another boxer from Australia, Paddy Slavin, for the Empire title, and had a chat with him.

Living so near Sydney, the cricket-mad boy had the chance to watch top-class games (even if it meant playing truant from school) and, not lacking in confidence, even to meet some of the players. Even better, he bowled at the nets to the tourists from England. This happened during the 1881–82 visit to Australia by a team captained by Alfred Shaw, the Nottinghamshire bowler. Sammy was practising with some other boys near the present Sydney ground when he noticed George Ulyett and Dick Barlow, the Yorkshire and Lancashire all-rounders, who were passing.

> I asked them if they would have a drink. It was a very hot day, and they said yes. I took them to the hotel, and asked what they would have. George said a small bottle of champagne (five shillings a bottle) and stout. Barlow chose ginger pop, which I also had. Luckily I had half a sovereign in my pocket. When we got to the ground I asked if I might bowl at the nets to Ulyett. 'Certainly, my boy.' He let me bowl him out after five minutes. He then went in first v. New South Wales and got 40 odd. I was sitting with the players when he got out. He stood me a bottle of ginger pop, and gave me ten shillings, at the same time remarking I had bowled him into form.

A few years later, when Ulyett was captaining the Players against the Gentlemen, Sammy bowled him in each innings.

Strangely, although Sammy was to play cricket on four continents and had a first-class career lasting a quarter of a century, this seems to be the nearest he came to playing on the famous ground in his native city. He certainly never played first-class cricket in Australia before leaving for England in his mid-teens; and although on a home visit at the time of the 1901–2 England tour he helped out in one or two upcountry matches he did not play in any major fixture. Probably he had another go at the nets at the Sydney ground during that tour (quite likely on the same occasion that 'Stringy Bark' put the wind up some of the England players), but an appearance on the ground eluded him. There is, though, a curious little story (to come later) of how he was to have played in a Test there, but never did.

The first big match he saw in Sydney was New South Wales v Victoria. Billy Murdoch, the Australian captain, scored 321. One memory Sammy had of him was that he did not go into lunch either day of his innings, but had a sandwich and glass of water sitting out in the sun. In later years Sammy would advise batsmen awaiting their turn at the wicket always to sit in front of the pavilion getting used to the light.

Later Sammy and his hero of that match were to meet on the cricket field more than once as rival county captains in England, the former leading Somerset and Murdoch Sussex. Sammy had played truant to watch the match and 'I got a jolly good caning each evening,' he said. 'Still, so keen on the game was I that I took three good canings and was perfectly satisfied with my lot.'

He also saw the Hon. Ivo Bligh's team which went to Australia in 1882–3 and avenged England's defeat by Murdoch's men at the Oval a few months earlier, which had led to the mock obituary in the *Sporting Times* 'in affectionate remembrance of English cricket' whose 'body will be cremated and the ashes taken to Australia.' Watching Bligh's X1 play in Sydney, Sammy little thought that in a very few years he would be playing in England in the company of some of these players.

Young Sammy's new hero at the time of Bligh's visit was a now forgotten Middlesex batsman called Charles Leslie, 'a fine light-haired young man . . . What delightful strokes he made.' He saw Leslie hit a century against New South Wales. Then, in the Test match which decided the series and took the Ashes back to England, Sammy backed him for threepence to score 50. Unfortunately the Australian

X1 included a fast bowler named Fred Spofforth, known as the Demon, an old boy of Sydney Grammar School. To Sammy's horror Spofforth sent the middle stump flying first ball with a yorker. The youngster was 'never so near crying over a cricket incident in my life.' Not because of the three-pence he lost, but because of his admiration for Leslie.

John Woods was an early enthusiast for bowls in the Sydney area, but the extent of his interest in cricket is not known. As one of the pioneers of Manly village, however, he was involved in the development of the excellent ground there known as the Oval. A Manly club was formed and among the famous cricketers who took part in challenge matches there in the next few years were Spofforth and Murdoch, as well as one in the making, Sammy Woods. Later Grace led an English team which played on the ground. Sammy's younger brother, Harris, was for a time Manly's captain.

Around this time John Woods had acquired Fairlight House, just west of Manly, where, it was recorded, his hospitable doors were constantly open to his many friends. Some had asked him to stand for Parliament, but his widespread business interests (which were to extend to cattle runs in Queensland) prevented him from accepting, although he did take some part in political affairs. Probably he also wanted to devote more time to his large family as he grew older; the last of his children, Campbell, being born in 1878.

Family photographs show a large, well-built man, heavily bearded; with a slightly forbidding countenance and clearly someone of strong character. Sammy remembered his father having been described as 'one of the strongest men who ever went to Australia'. He also felt he was one of the most humorous, and recalled:

> Three of us boys asked to learn the cornet. Father bought us one each, and engaged a professor to teach us. We practised in the stables about 300 yards from the house, and after about three months we were all playing 'Killarney'. One night father said, 'Now, boys, I hear you can play a tune. Take the boat and row out half a mile and the one who plays it best will have a sovereign.' I won it. Perhaps I played loudest.

The English wicketkeeper, Dick Lilley, who was in MacLaren's 1901–2 party, met John Woods more than once when the tourists played in Sydney and received 'a very cordial welcome' from him and

14

his sons. Mr Woods senior, he recalled, was 'a fine old gentleman, and one did not need to be long in his company to discover what a splendid old sportsman he was, too . . . By knowing Mr Woods, one was better able to appreciate the source whence S.M.J. obtained his best sporting instincts.'

The Sydney in which Sammy grew up was a fast-changing city. Its population had doubled between the time his parents had arrived from Ireland and his birth, and then doubled again before his schooldays there were over. The harbour presented an animated scene, and Sammy and his brothers must have gazed many times on the great woolclippers from England. Among them was the *Cutty Sark*, which had made the long journey in under 10 weeks. Visitors in the 1870s were moved not only by the beauty of the harbour but by the business activity and growth of Sydney, to which John Woods was making a not negligible contribution.

There was 'an air of solid prosperity' about Sydney, one wrote at this time, with the business area being rapidly rebuilt, with 'commercial palaces, equal to those in London' and fine public buildings, also with a British appearance. The better-off, like the Woods family, had their fine houses; but the city also had its vile slums, as bad as any back in the 'home country'. For Britain was still very much 'home', and there was a British-ness about the social life, morality, and etiquette, at least at the level at which the Woods lived.

When Sammy was 16, his father decided to send him, with brother Harris, who was 18 months younger, to complete his education in England. Now although Sammy's sporting prowess was obvious enough, he was not nearly as interested in classroom lessons, and why John took this decision to spend a great deal of money in sending him to a public school and university thousands of miles away is not obvious. The university in Sydney was by now well established. Perhaps, as has been suggested, father's hope was to make Sammy and Harris into 'English gentlemen'. Whatever the reason, the decision was taken, and plans were made for the great journey.

The Suez Canal had brought Australia and England a little closer, but John Woods chose a long journey, perhaps for business reasons, perhaps to see a bit more of the world, including a visit to China. Sammy, in his reminiscences, never wasted words on describing his many long sea voyages (he must have spent not far short of a year of his life at sea, including his various cricket tours and war service). It is known, though, from the envious comments of fellow cricketers who suffered sea-sickness that he, at least, was a good sailor. He would eat well and smoke his favourite cigars, the smell of which did not ease their suffering.

Of this boyhood journey halfway round the world, Sammy records only 'a funny thing' that happened on the way to Shanghai:

> We ran into a Chinese fishing fleet at night, and crashed into several frail wooden craft. They hadn't any lights. Well, some of them clambered aboard, and sorry wretches they looked. Still they had to be helped overboard again.

The vessel the Woods were travelling in sailed up the Yangtse-Kiang to Hankow, where they waited to ship tea before resuming their voyage. This, Sammy thought, was 'the most beautiful river in the world', compared to which the Nile, which he travelled on much later, was 'the most over-rated stretch of water in existence'.

At about this time it is known that John Woods visited not only China but also, briefly, India while on the way to Europe. Probably this was on the same journey, though Sammy does not mention India. Woods senior was also to go on to visit Germany, France, and Austria, and, ever the far-sighted business man, became a partner in a large bacon-curing business in the western part of England. Probably, too, it was at this time that he cemented a friendship with an English banker named Burrington who was to play a significant role in Sammy's next few years, acting as a kind of guardian and, indirectly, leading to Sammy's forsaking his native land.

A New Country

It was to be more than four years before Sammy entered Cambridge University and almost immediately find himself called up for Test cricket by the Australian tourists. By then he had made his name as one of the outstanding public-school cricketers of his day, and had already made his first-class debut for a South of England XI against the 1886 Australian team. He had also, before going to Cambridge, had his introduction to English county cricket with Somerset; then still a second-class county, but not, with his help, for much longer.

There was also, between school and university, a brief taste of working for a living, as a bank clerk. It was one of the fortunately few interruptions in a life otherwise devoted to cricket, rugby, soccer, hockey, golf, bowls, hunting, shooting, racing, skittles, snooker, and one or two other pastimes. He preferred always to be a player, but next best was to be a spectator or just to talk and talk about sport and sportsmen over 'a gargle', as he put it, in club, pub, hotel bar, or one of the country houses in which he was always a welcome guest.

The public school at which Sammy and Harris were perhaps to be fashioned into gentlemen was Brighton College. First, however, there were a few months at Silwood House, Tunbridge Wells, which Sammy referred to as 'a preparatory school' and which in the town directory described itself as 'a gentlemen's school'. One wonders if there could have been a bigger and older pupil than the confident 16-year-old from down under.

There is little record of his life at this time, but the brothers would have found the genteel town on the Kent-Sussex border a great contrast to the busy, fast-growing Sydney they had left behind. Tunbridge Wells (the Royal was not added until a quarter of a centruy later by Edward VII) had long been a fashionable spa for visitors, with its bath house and many elegant buildings. Now it was becoming increasingly a residential town.

But boys of this age are very adaptable, and Sammy more than most had little trouble in making himself at home. More important to

17

him than the famous colonnaded Pantiles and the other architectural and historic delights of the town was the cricket. It had been played at Tunbridge Wells long before the first transported convicts arrived at what was to become Sydney. Kent played a match or two in the town for many years, and only a year or two before the Woods boys arrived an Australian XI had met an England XI there.

Sammy's only reference in his reminiscences to his days in the town was about cricket:

> Whilst at Tunbridge Wells I played cricket for the Town club, and on a few occasions went in first with A.F.J. Ford, a mighty hitter. Twice we put up 100 for the first wicket. My share of the runs were few, as I was a very steady little bat at the time.

For the first time 'S. Woods' was appearing regularly in a newspaper, and gradually rose in the batting order. At the end of the 1884 season when the *Kent and Sussex Courier* published the club's batting averages, Sammy's name was seventh out of a large number who had played that season. His average was 17.2, his highest score 42 not out. He took a few wickets, too, but no bowling averages appeared – indeed, strangely, bowling figures were not often considered worth publishing in those days.

That August, just before he started at Brighton College, Sammy saw his first big cricket match in England. Although it ended as a draw it was, as he said, a good one to start with. It was the Oval Test, much written about since, in which all eleven home players bowled as the Australians scored 551, with Murdoch hitting the first double century in the history of Test cricket. For the first time Sammy saw underarm bolwing, the England wicketkeeper, the Hon. Alfred Lyttleton, in fact proving the most successful bowler with his lobs. He took four wickets for 19 runs, one of the victims being caught by the substitute keeper, W.G. Grace.

Brighton College, standing on high ground in the Kemp Town district and not far from the sea, had been founded 40 years earlier by some prominent local residents to provide 'a thoroughly liberal and practical education in conformity with the principles of the Established Church'. Whatever other benefits it may have given the young Australian, it had, in the words of the weekly journal *Cricket* a year or two later, 'the distinction of playing an important part in the cricket education of one of the most promising all-round players of today'.

Some of his achievements on the cricket field there make incredible reading over a century later. But although he had a few unimportant games as soon as he started that autumn, it was quickly football weather. And then: 'What a pack of misery I was when I found out that the school game was soccer and not rugby.'

Being a big boy Sammy was selected in the first trial game to play at centre-half, and found himself opposing another future impressive all-round sportsman, George Cotterill, at centre-forward. Cotterill 'was captain of everything', and later played soccer for England and cricket for Sussex. Of their first encounter, Sammy recalled that 'the ball was in the air, and one could charge in those days. He did, and knocked me flying. I have never seen so many stars.'

Soon Sammy found himself in goal – 'having played rugby in Australia I could naturally catch the ball, and I could punt' – and very soon was not only in the school team but was playing for Sussex against London at the Oval. London fielded no fewer than nine internationals. There was, however, a lot of talent in the Sussex team, which won 2–1 and soon afterwards drew 1–1 with the unbeaten Cambridge team, also at the Oval. Again the following winter he played for Sussex, now as a full-back.

At Christmas Sammy spent the holiday in Dorset, at Sherborne: perhaps with school friends, or possibly with some business associate of his father (the bacon-curing firm in which John Woods had acquired an interest was at Gillingham, only a few miles away). Sammy had been brought up on a pony in Australia and loved riding, and he spent this and the following Christmas hunting with the Blackmore Vale. 'How I loved it,' he recalled. 'Never shall I forget the glorious runs we had. In the famous run from Jack White's Gibbet my horse hit a gate and knocked me out.'

But cricket he loved most of all. In his two summers at Brighton the college had one of the strongest school teams of the time. They were unbeaten in 11 games in his first year and lost only two out of 12 in the second. Apart from Sammy, gathering pace and accuracy as a bowler, there were Cotterill and one or two other very promising players, Leslie Gay and G.L. (Billy) Wilson. Gay later played cricket for Somerset and Hampshire and both cricket and soccer for England; and Wilson, a countryman of Sammy's, played for Sussex and, back in Australia, a game or two for Victoria.

There was also Harris Woods. Overshadowed by his slightly older brother, he was a useful player and had a game for Somerset in their second-class days. Sammy indeed later ranked his brother as the best cover point he had ever seen, with the exception of the great Gilbert Jessop, 'and nearly as good at hitting the stumps at the bowler's end'.

Sammy, usually batting at No. 3, came second to Cotterill in the batting honours, with an average of 36 over the two summers. He topped the bowling, with 59 wickets at just over 8 apiece the first year and 78 for 7.3 the second, averaging a wicket every 20 deliveries. He was worshipped by his fellow pupils. One of them, E.J. Oakley, who fagged for him, recalled: 'Though no scholar, Sammy was popular with everyone, masters and boys alike, and to the boys he was a hero, and although his exuberant spirits and superabundant vitality led him into many a scrape, he never made an enemy.'

He also left a glimpse of the cricketer: 'To see Sammy coming out of the pavilion with his cheerful grin and stop the rot by his favourite method of 'tip and run', with an occasional hit of a loose ball clean out of the ground, was a sight for the gods.'

The college report for Sammy's first season, in rather more favourable terms than that on his academic progress, said: 'Bats in a rather peculiar style, but with great success; his late cutting being very pretty. His bowling, very fast and straight, did great execution, and was the chief cause of the great success of the season. His fielding is excellent.'

Sammy's most memorable innings at Brighton College was when he hit 205 for the college XI against the Next 16, including masters and professionals. 'It was hard to get the ball through so many fielders,' he said. But as spectacular as his batting could be, it was as a bowler that he was most feared, beating the bat with his sheer pace. 'No one was able to make any stand against the splendid bowling of Woods,' said a report of one of his first matches, at Dulwich, when he took 6 for 17 (perhaps he could also claim a seventh victim, since another batsman 'retired hurt').

A remarkable feature of his bowling was the number of times he hit the stumps. His outstanding performance was at Lancing College in his second year, when he took 8 for 17 (all bowled) and 6 for 10 (five bowled, one caught and bowled).

On another occasion Sammy is said to have hit the stumps eight times in succession in a single five-ball over. (Although the five-ball over did not become law until 1889, it was already in use in many matches, including, it seems, at Brighton College.) There were three no-balls and twice he hit the stumps without dislodging a bail, so all he got was three wickets. This incredible over has been referred to in print several times, yet there is no reference to it in any of the

20

contemporary accounts of matches in the Brighton College magazine. A hat-trick is recorded here; three wickets in four balls there; and in another match he took wickets with consecutive deliveries on three occasions. Neither does Sammy himself mention the eight in eight balls in his reminiscences (although he also omits many other achievements). In an interview in *The Cricket Field* in 1892 he recalled his seven wickets in seven deliveries at school in Sydney and also, playing for Brighton College against Dulwich he remembered 'hitting the leg stump – and hitting it hard – three times in one over, without knocking the bails off.' He added: 'As though this were not bad enough every ball went for four byes.'

His victims were not only fellow schoolboys. One of the strong sides Brighton played in his first summer was an M.C.C. and Ground team, and Sammy was delighted to get the wicket (one of his six) of a member of the Hearne family of professional cricketers. He claimed it with an unexpected delivery.

Sammy recalled that earlier he had gone to watch Sussex play Surrey, and:

> It was then that I saw George Lohmann bowl for the first time and saw him c. and b. W. Newham with a slow ball after that batsman had got over a hundred. I never forgot this, and that very evening I started practising a slow ball at the nets until it was dark. This ball meant very much to me in years to come, for I hardly ever bowled three consecutive overs unless I tried a slow one. In the very first match after this I got my first victim, 'G.G. Hearne c. and b. Woods 48'. He had played through the innings for the M.C.C., and it was the first slow ball I ever bowled. Still, it took me some time before I could trust myself to bowl it.

Up to this time he had bowled with little variation, mainly being content with sheer pace. He told an interviewer a few years later he had 'always had a strained side', and added: 'If it were not for that I should bowl very much faster.' He was fast enough. More than once (a contemporary recalled) the school wicketkeeper, standing 10 yards back, fielded a flying stump.

Sammy was 19 when he left Brighton College at the end of the summer term of 1886 (returning for a few matches for the Old Brightonians), and that August he played his first first-class match. It was for G.N. Wyatt's XI against the Australians.

Wyatt was a dashing batsman who had played in turn for Gloucestershire and Surrey before finishing his first-class career that year with Sussex. He had mostly Sussex players in what was termed his South of England XI for the encounter with the tourists at Portsmouth. There were three Australians in the team: Sammy; his schoolmate, Billy Wilson, who was still only 18; and Claude Rock, already a Cambridge Blue, who played for Warwickshire in the days before it joined the first-class counties and later for his native Tasmania.

Also playing was a young Sussex bowler, soon to captain the county and lead the first England team to South Africa: C. Aubrey Smith, later to become more widely known as a Hollywood film actor. He and Sammy were already acquainted, having played soccer for Sussex together.

The Australian team, led on this tour by Dr. Henry Scott, had a fairly comfortable victory, dismissing Wyatt's men (and new boys) for 183 and 187 and winning by seven wickets. Sammy, however, could be reasonably satisfied with his debut against first-class opposition, which included the Demon Spofforth. Going in at No. 9 he scored 21, putting on 35 for the wicket with Smith; and hitting 11 in the second innings. He opened the bowling and took 2 for 45 in 33 overs, both victims being clean bowled, and 0 for 40. He strained his side through trying to bowl too fast, otherwise he 'would have done better', he felt.

That same month saw Sammy living in Somerset, and it was here, apart from his years at Cambridge and in the Army in the 1914–18 war, that he was to spend the rest of his life. Not that he or the friends he quickly made there expected it at the time.

The town he lived in first and for many years, and for which he always had a great affection, was Bridgwater, a strong contrast to Tunbridge Wells and Brighton. Its two claims to fame are what is said to be the world's biggest illuminated carnival, held through the streets every November; and the last battle on English soil, fought three miles away on Sedgemoor after the rebellious citizens of Bridgwater and Taunton had crowned as 'king' the Duke of Monmouth, Charles II's first and favourite bastard.

A small mainly working-class town with a strong streak of independence (and a hint of disdain for the county town of Taunton a few miles further inland), Bridgwater had a then-busy river harbour and brickmaking industry; and a passion for rugby. Sammy seems to have had little problem in making himself very much at home here and involving himself in the life of the town. In years to come he was to ride in splendour in the carnival as its chairman.

The connection with Bridgwater came about through a warm friendship his father had formed, through business dealings, with Gilbert George Burrington, a member of a local family who was, among other things, the leading figure in the town's cricket club.

Burrington, although only in his early thirties, had been the 'genial and highly respected' manager of Fox, Fowler and Co's bank since it opened in Bridgwater a few years earlier. Described in a contemporary report also as 'a very keen man of business', he was associated in his long service as a banker with several companies and was director of at least one. The nature of the business which brought him into contact with Sammy's father is obscure, but they seem to have quickly hit it off together. The trust that John Woods placed in the Somerset banker was such that when he returned to New South Wales he was happy to leave Burrington as a kind of guardian to young Sammy and also, presumably, brother Harris.

The important thing for Sammy's future was that Burrington, too, had a great love of cricket. He had helped to galvanise new life into the moribund Bridgwater Cricket Club. Its ground, on the western outskirts of the town, was only a short distance from the Burrington home, Westfield House, which old photographs show to have been a substantial residence whose grounds included a tennis court.

Doubtless Burrington dug into his own pocket to help the cricket club to better days. His influence and interest brought to the town several well-known touring sides of the time, and even two-day matches were played. He was also, again of importance to the course of Sammy's life, a keen supporter of the Somerset county club, and served for a time on its committee. He captained the Bridgwater team and was a useful if not outstanding player, best known for the wickets he claimed with some wily slow underhand bowling. His contribution to the game, however, was not measured by his wickets. A cricket correspondent of the day wrote that 'he was a keen and genuine sportsman, setting an example of work which his suave and gentlemanly personality rendered difficult to resist.'

It was not long before Sammy was introduced to the sporting life of Bridgwater, and he was soon turning out for the cricket club and also the town's rugby XV.

Sammy's achievements on the cricket field were quickly known to the county club (Burrington, no doubt, made sure of that) and he was invited to play in their final match of the 1886 season. The date was

August 26, the place Birmingham, and the opponents Warwickshire, then a second-class county like Somerset. (Although some of its friendly matches against leading counties in the early 1880s have been awarded first-class status, Somerset did not really become a first-class club until the next decade.) This was the first of over 300 matches, nearly all first-class, that Sammy was to play for Somerset over almost a quarter of a century.

It was an auspicious debut. Somerset won by 83 runs in a low-scoring match, largely due to Sammy's bowling, and not at all to his batting. He opened the innings and in each was dismissed for 0 (his only other pair in a county match was to be against Yorkshire).

But if there was not even one of the favourite scampered singles to announce his arrival on the county scene, he made his name at once when he took the ball. With the first delivery he claimed the wicket of his fellow Australian, Rock. Sammy never forgot to give credit to the wicketkeeper.

A fellow player, William Roe, recorded the moment: 'It was a terrifically fast yorker on the leg side. Rock missed it and was stumped by A.E. Newton. It was one of the very finest bits of stumping I have ever seen.' Newton, standing right up to the wicket despite Sammy's pace, took the ball left-handed and whipped off the bails.

It was not only a fine piece of stumping, it was also the first of many wickets Sammy owed to Arthur Newton. An Old Etonian and Oxford Blue, whose career with Somerset lasted even a decade longer than Sammy's, Newton was still playing in club cricket in his early 80s.

Rock got his revenge by bowling Sammy in the second innings, but when Warwickshire batted again Sammy was once more his downfall – with a bad ball. It was a slow delivery which bounced twice and yorked the batsman with the second bounce! Sammy (according to Roe) swore that he had bowled a double bouncer on purpose, as Rock seemed able to play any other kind of ball, but of course no one believed him.

Sammy's figures in the match were 7 for 23 and 5 for 34: 12 wickets for under five runs apiece. Nearly half his 44 overs were maidens.

The next issue of the *Somerset County Gazette* praised the bowling of the young Australian, but added that 'the less said of his qualification [to play for Somerset] the better, perhaps.' However, it was not a time when qualifications were taken too seriously, and even many years later, when amateurs still predominated in the county game and it was sometimes hard to get a side together, no one looked too closely. In the 1920s the future New Zealand captain, Tom Lowry, qualified for Somerset, it was said, by having come from Wellington; although an enquirer would soon have discovered it was not the Wellington near Taunton. It was also enough for the Somerset all-rounder and cricket writer, R.C. Robertson-Glasgow, to have had cousins at Hinton Charterhouse, one of them M.P. for Bath.

The *Sussex Daily News* of August 31, recording Sammy's match-winning performance at Birmingham, referred to those 'who [had] anticipated or hoped that he would ultimately render good service to Sussex.' It also mentioned, by way of explanation of Sammy's choice of county that 'the guardian of the young Australian' (Burrington) lived in Somerset.

The Somerset county newspaper also reported at the same time: 'Mr Woods is obtaining an insight into the banking business at Bridgwater, and will probably next year return to his native country.' This raises doubts as to whether his entry into university was by any means certain at that point, especially as his time at Brighton must have confirmed him as a unlikely scholar. But certainly he was now learning the banking business, either in the branch managed by his 'guardian', or one of the other two banks then in the same town. It was in fact another year and a half before Sammy went to Cambridge, and in his reminiscences he recalled:

> My father intimated, being a great business man, that I had better learn business habits before I went up. I did. I went into a Bank for six or seven months. You know, opened the door, kept the stamp book, shut the desks; that is, when I wasn't playing cricket or football.

Sammy was never any good with money, as his account of how the banking world lost his services shows:

> I left over the stamp-book. We were balancing, and an inspector asked me why I hadn't balanced the same. I explained we didn't do so. I told him that when I wanted stamps I got a sovereign from the cashier and bought a pound's worth. When they were finished I got another sovereign and got some more. It used to be sixpence postage to Australia in those days, and as I didn't often write home

to mother, I didn't think there was a lot to complain about, and I told him to get someone else to keep the book. As they hadn't paid me a bob, and I had got them several farmers' accounts, I really think it was their loss, not mine.

Sammy then embarked on the next – and briefest – of his careers, which he laconically recorded thus:

> I then paid a man £50 to teach me land surveying. We went out with a chain the first afternoon and measured some ground. Something to do with roods, perches, etc. He went to Bristol that night with my £50, and stayed there a week, then he went home and shot himself with a rifle. Whether he had had too much to drink or not, I don't know. All I know is, it wouldn't be expedient for anyone to pay me for measuring a plot of ground.

His only other attempt to earn a living came a few years later when he was on the payroll of a Somerset brewery, which for the hard-drinking man he became was a little more understandable than the 'home' he had for a time in Bridgwater. This was the George Hotel, in George Street, offering 'every comfort at moderate charges' to families and commercial gentlemen. The George was, in fact, a temperance hotel. Sammy was of such a gregarious nature, however, that he was probably rarely at 'home' there in the room or rooms he rented. Sadly, it would seem, he was never to have a proper home of his own, living in hotels, clubs, rooms in public houses, and, often, as a welcome guest in the houses of his many friends. It is doubtful, too, if he ever accumulated many material possessions: his cricket and rugby gear would have been the most important.

Rugby was (and is) Bridgwater's first sport, and for many years it supplied the nucleus of the Somerset XV. Sammy was usually a threequarter at this time, and he remembered 'two wonderful seasons' when the club lost only one match. He was drafted into the Somerset team for its first northern tour, and wrote:

> I was at full-back versus Lancashire on the Saturday, and before 15,000 people I made two awful mistakes, and they got two tries. I was shifted to wing threequarter. A scrimmage was formed near the half-way line. The half-back,

F.H. Fox, sent me the ball. I put it over the bar with my left foot, which made up for the other mistakes, and as we got two splendid tries afterwards we won. How furious the Northern papers were over Lancashire's defeat. I remember reading one account of the match, and it was, 'Where the 'ell is Somerset?'

But the other match, against Yorkshire, ended in defeat.

Sammy played forward after this, and in February 1888 got his South cap. At the time England were involved in a dispute with the other rugby unions and as a result were not playing, so only an 'imaginary XV' was picked. Sammy was surprised and upset not to be chosen. Playing for the South he had stayed in the game despite a bad cut from a kick over the eye, later suffering concussion. So he 'was very sick in more ways than one'.

In the summer of 1887 there was plenty of cricket for Sammy with Bridgwater ('lots of runs and wickets,' including two centuries) and other clubs (four wickets in four balls for Wellington). He remembered enjoying 'some of the jolliest cricket I ever had' with Bridgwater. 'Thorough sportsmen they were,' he recalled long after, 'and men who made a day of a match on a Saturday. Not like the present club cricket, "When is the next train home?"'

In one match for Bridgwater against a strong Somerset Club and Ground side he took 16 wickets for 77. He also played in the first of many country-house matches, often of a high standard, and at the magnificent Quantock Lodge ground hit 167. More important, he was now establishing himself as a very promising member of the county team.

One match for Somerset he recalled was at Southampton, where Hampshire's Sam Forster, who never progressed to the first-class game, hit him out of the ground four times.

> I remember I got up early the day of the match as I saw some young men playing cricket on the common outside our hotel. I had a bath and joined in. I got four wickets and scored 25 before breakfast. I came in rather hot. Someone at breakfast said, 'You seem very hot, what have you been doing?' 'Having a practice for today's game,' I replied. In that game v. Hants. I got 20 and 24 and got 10 wickets. Nothing like practice, is there?

Sammy played against Grace for the first time that season when Somerset travelled to Cheltenham. He should have had the great man's wicket first ball, but the catch was missed. Grace went on to make 'over 90 of the best' on a wet wicket. That season Sammy was Somerset's top wicket-taker, with 37 victims at just over 18 runs each, and with the bat he averaged 23.

That same summer he also played at Lord's against the M.C.C. It was the first time he had seen the ground, and he met more of the leading players of the day. He was keen to improve his game and to take note of what they were saying. Sammy was soon to be counted among them as an equal, but he never pretended to know it all and was always eager to learn. He believed in the importance of youngsters watching and studying, and was against too much coaching. Many years later when he himself coached schoolboys, 'I didn't say twenty words to them in an hour.'

Apart from learning and improving his game, whether cricket or rugby, Sammy was also getting to know this new part of the world and its people: the seemingly slow Somerset folk whose manner of speech and idiom he was to use more and more himself. He was also coming to love the green hills and fertile vales of the county. To the west of the main road between Bridgwater and Taunton rose the Quantock Hills. Much later he wrote:

> I have been in most parts of the world, but better scenery I have never seen. From the top one can look across the Bristol Channel valley, and on the other you see the Brendon Hills, Exmoor, and the lovely Minehead Valley. In each valley we grow the best wheat and barley in the world; and in each valley live the best sportsmen in the west.

Over the years Sammy often walked the hills. One of the most often told anecdotes concerns his caches of Somerset ale or cider concealed in hedges and hollow trees at strategic points in the Quantocks. On a hot day he would suddenly produce a bottle or two to the astonishment of his companion on the walk. He was similarly said to have hidden refreshment here and there among the sand dunes on the famous Burnham golf links, where he often played.

Gilbert Jessop, the giant of Gloucester cricket, vouched for the truth of these stories and recorded in print his own first acquaintance with what he called Sammy's 'famous bottle trick'. The two had been walking in the Quantocks and were far from habitation when Sammy proposed a halt for a drink. 'With no signs of that commodity in sight, I termed this a sorry joke,' recalled Jessop. Whereupon Sammy produced a bottle or two from a burrow. At the end of the walk there was even better to come when a bottle of champagne was lifted from a pond.

'The Jolliest Years'

In 1888 Sammy started his innings at Cambridge and he recalled his time there as 'four of the jolliest years I have had in my life'. He entered Jesus College, where 'my companions were about eighteen of the very best of fellows, who all gained Blues of one sort or another, some of us being double Blues'. It was indeed a golden age for cricket, football, and other sports at Jesus.

Sammy was soon elected to two clubs, the Rhadegund and the Natives, the former a port wine club (founded, the college history says, 'for leading athletes') and the latter an oyster club. In due course he became president of each and, he remembered, 'What lovely times these were, with a sing song at each of our meetings!' Cricket, rugby, and a social life with like-minded companions were the ingredients of those 'jolliest years', in which academic study played an insignificant part. There were also some foolhardy incidents which it is perhaps charitable to regard as mere pranks by high-spirited undergraduates.

Oxford had turned Sammy down, it was said, not realising his sporting prowess, and were to rue the decision. Oxford lost three of the four varsity matches in those years (rain saved them in the other). Their average innings was only just over 100, and only once did an Oxford batsman get beyond the 30s. Sammy took 36 wickets (19 bowled, four caught and bowled) for under nine runs apiece. These figures and his performances in many other first-class matches in the Cambridge years (including a hat-trick in one and all 10 wickets in an innings in another) explain why, a century later, he is still remembered as one of the very greatest bowlers to have represented the university.

In the first year, at only 21, he established himself as a regular choice for the Gentlemen against the Players, a fixture regarded as almost as important as a Test match. And it was in 1888 also that he himself became a Test player. In *Giants of the Game*, the Hon. R.H. Lyttleton wrote: 'Few players have made such a name for themselves in so short a time.'

Sammy had taken £10 to £2 that he got a double Blue in his first year, and he had no problem in gaining that. It was only a question of whether it would be cricket and rugby or cricket and soccer, and he chose the former. A broken collarbone in his first game at Cambridge did not prevent his quickly gaining his rugby Blue; and he got his colours at Jesus College for both codes of football.

A couple of years later, a chapter on John Woods in *Australian Men of Mark* concluded with a brief reference to the sporting success then being achieved by 'his son Samuel' at Cambridge, and went on to say he 'also has done well in the intellectual life of the place'. Sammy (Samuel sounds wrong) would have had one of his loud laughs at that. It was a bit of wishful thinking on the part of father, or perhaps the author had thought it a safe thing to add. Or, dare we wonder, had Sammy, in letters home, given a somewhat false impression of his progress? (Father, after all, was footing a not inconsiderable bill for these jolly times.) There had been, in black and white, in the newly launched university paper, *The Granta*, the evidence that in a poll of readers Sammy had failed by a mere half a dozen votes to have been chosen as the cleverest man in Cambridge. But that, of course, was only an undergraduate joke.

Sammy had no pretensions to scholarship, and joked about it. He once told his fellow Somerset cricketer, Roe: 'Of course I know that 4 and 5 make 8, but whether 8 and 7 make 14 or 13 I can't for the life of me remember'. It was also said that he was well on in life before he read a novel (it was *Oliver Twist*, which he much enjoyed). The cricket writer, Sir Home Gordon, a friend of Sammy's, observed once that 'grey matter was not predominant in his powerful physique'. Perhaps a little unkind, for Sammy was far from stupid. It was just that he was devoted solely to the pursuit of his pleasures, which were those of the playing field. They did not include study.

It was the same friend who recalled Sammy's telling him in later days: 'There is one thing I have steadily tried to do: to drink more beer for the years I have lived than any other man who has ever come down from Cambridge.' Sammy claimed to be the only under-graduate who had gone to breakfast with the Master of Jesus College, 'Black' Morgan, and asked for beer – which he got.

There was nothing backward about Sammy when it came to audacity. During the first summer at Cambridge the Dean's wife gave a garden party, at which a cornet player was playing 'Killarney'. Sammy took possession of the instrument and was playing 'vilely', as he himself put it, before being stopped. This was more audacious than may at first seem, for the Dean was 'Red' Morgan, an enormous man and masterful character. Everyone was afraid of him, including, it was

31

said, the Master (the two were unrelated, and their nicknames derived from the colour of their hair). Sammy was in trouble with the Dean more than once, but recalled that 'it didn't last long' and 'Red' Morgan would conclude an interview with: 'Well, the best of luck at Lord's!'

Examinations were the only things to mar those years at Cambridge. One often-told story is that when taking a paper all that a worried Sammy wrote was his name and college at the top of a sheet: 'S.M.J. Woods, Jesus'; and that one word of that was wrongly spelt. Certainly he was not good at spelling: in his will there was a mistake in the names of two of the three beneficiaries, one of them a sister.

His lack of success with his studies reached the point where his continued residence at Cambridge was in serious doubt. He may have been a double Blue and by now a Test cricketer, and he may have collected an England rugby cap or two, but towards the end of 1890 the Jesus dons had decided that unless Sammy passed his 'Little Go' he must be sent down.

A contemporary has left an amusing account of the time when the hero of the sports field faced his greatest test. Writing under the pseudonym of 'Country Vicar', the Rev. R.L. Hodgson recalled in one of his cricket books the consternation among other undergraduates at the possibility of losing Sammy. None could do anything to help: it was impossible to impersonate such a well-known figure and take his place.

That October Hodgson, then a nervous freshman just 'up', made his way to the Corn Exchange, the scene of the 'Little Go'. Among the many others making their way was 'a great, broadshouldered figure, with a shock of thick hair and lean, sun-burnt face. He wore a short and somewhat tattered gown – an ancient college cap.' Someone said, 'That's Sammy Woods!' And Hodgson 'gazed, in humble admiration, at the towering form stalking moodily in front of us'.

In the days that followed, sitting facing the great man, Hodgson observed his unhappiness. He appeared to write little, sitting there biting his quill pen, with a 'depressed and gloomy countenance'. He seldom remained in the Corn Exchange longer than the obligatory period of about half an hour. Then he strode forth 'looking black as thunder'. They were probably the least jolly moments of his life.

There was, however, one hope. Two of the examiners were noted sportsmen: H.G. Fuller, president of the rugby club, and the Rev J.H. Gray, treasurer of the cricket club. Could they prevent the calamity?

'The answer', wrote Hodgson, 'is still unknown, although there were certain suspicions that something was done.'

Never did a 'Little Go' list excite such interest. The undergraduates were almost as much interested in a name at the bottom as in their own. And there is was: 'Woods, S.M.J.' – in class IV of parts 1 and 2. All was well!

Cambridge folklore includes a couple of other versions, at least one apocryphal, of that 'something' which was done to ensure Sammy's survival. A *viva voce* examination was arranged, and, it was said, Sammy was asked: 'What was the name of the first king of Israel?' After long cogitation, he replied: 'Saul'. 'Thank you, Mr Woods, that will be all.' As Sammy left, the heady wine of erudition went surging to his head. He turned and triumphantly added: 'Which was also called Paul'.

And there is this version:

> First examiner: 'And who, Mr. Woods, led the Israelites out of Egypt?'
> Long silence from a puzzled Sammy.
> Second examiner: 'Then who was Aaron's brother?'
> Further silence, then:
> Third examiner: 'Mr Woods, do you not even know your own middle name?'
> Sammy (light dawning): Moses!

Sammy had swiftly made his mark at cricket that spring and summer of 1888, which proved a wet season. In the Freshman's match early in May he starred as a batsman, making 13 (out of only 38) and then 98; but disappointed with his bowling, although he took seven wickets. But then he got into his stride and started claiming lots of wickets, and knew he would get his Blue.

Before May was out he had taken 12 wickets in a match twice, against the Gentlemen of England and against Yorkshire, both of whom Cambridge defeated, largely due to his efforts. He hit 60 and took six wickets against the M.C.C. and Ground, and stood behind the stumps for most of the second innings when the wicketkeeper was hurt. It was against the Gentlemen on May 17 that he achieved his only first-class hat-trick (although there were others in club cricket). The visitors were led by Charles Inglis Thornton, the greatest hitter of the day, who played first for Kent and then for Middlesex. More than once on his visits to Cambridge he was to hit Sammy out of

Fenner's. Most of the other Gentlemen on this occasion were also Middlesex men.

This was only the third first-class match in which Sammy had played (he had had none in 1887). The hat-trick came in the Gentlemen's first innings, when they were dismissed for only 79. Sammy took 7 for 48 in 19 four-ball overs. The three batsmen who fell to consecutive deliveries, all useful wickets to get, were P.J. de Paravicini (bowled), Thornton (caught), and Perceval Henery (bowled). All were not only Middlesex men but, as it happened, Cambridge Blues. In the second innings Sammy claimed another five victims. It is not recorded if he was presented with a hat by the other players in recognition of his feat, as was sometimes the case in Victorian times.

That season he topped the averages for both the Cambridge batting (thanks to a few not outs) and bowling. With the bat he never failed to reach double figures until the varsity match at Lord's. This was the victim of atrocious weather, and although because of the rain it was agreed to play over four days instead of two, Oxford were unable to start their second innings. In the first Oxford had been dismissed for 124, with Sammy, opening the bowling, taking 6 for 48 in 39 overs, and on the final day would have needed 218 to win – a remote target – had the rain not returned. It was the first drawn match for over 40 years.

In less than two weeks, on July 16, Sammy was back at Lord's, this time as a member of the Australian XI for the first Test. A member of the tour party, Sam Jones, an all-rounder from Sydney, had contracted smallpox and missed most of the matches. The nature of his illness was concealed for fear it would lead to the tour being cancelled. Jones, also an old boy of Sydney Grammar School, was a fast-medium bowler, and to take his place the Australians (who had only 13 in the party) called up Sammy. So at the age of 21, with no first-class experience in his own country and only half a dozen or so first-class appearances in England, he stepped on to the international stage.

His debut match went into the record books, thanks to the weather. Because of heavy overnight rain, it did not start until 3 pm on the first day, and on the second 27 wickets fell in just over three hours on the mud pitch. It was all over before half past four, with the Australians victors by 61 runs. The scores: Australia 116 and 60, England 53 and 62. The total runs (291) remained the lowest for any completed Test until the 1930s.

Sammy's contribution was modest. Batting at No. 6 he scored 18 and 3 (yet only four of the other 21 players totalled more). His bowling was hardly needed. All but two of the England wickets fell to Charlie Turner − Turner the 'Terror' − and Jack Ferris, both from New South Wales, who formed one of cricket's great bowling duos. They bowled unchanged in both innings, excepting for four overs when Sammy took over from Ferris. Two of Sammy's overs were maidens, and he claimed one wicket for six runs. (The other England wicket was a run out). Sammy also took a superb one-handed catch at cover-point to dismiss Grace. 'Hard luck, old son!' the brash Australian newcomer called to the great man as he departed for the pavilion.

The other Tests, at the Oval and Manchester, were also over in two days, with England winning both by an innings after having won the toss. The rain again played its part, and England had the better of the wickets. At Old Trafford 18 wickets fell before lunch on the second day on a sticky wicket and the match ended before 2 o'clock in just over six and a half hours of playing time. Australia were all out in their second innings in little more than an hour for just 70 runs. When Sammy came to the crease Australia had lost five wickets with six runs on the board. He was bowled first ball.

Sammy's three appearances in Tests for Australia produced disappointing figures, though apart from Ferris and Turner none of the tourists distinguished themselves. He scored 32 runs in six innings, and took five wickets (four bowled) at an average of 24.2. He was in fact the only Australian wicket-taker other than the deadly duo. He also took part in a couple of other matches for the tourists, claiming another half a dozen wickets.

Sammy never played Test cricket for Australia again, although it would doubtless have been a different story had he gone back to live in his native country. He was to have played for the tourists against England when they returned two years later, in 1890, but was handicapped by injury. His next matches at international level were to be *for* England. According to 'Country Vicar', Sammy had actually been invited to play for England in the 1888 series as a result of his remarkable early performances at Cambridge, but declined because he was an Australian.

Apart from his matches for Cambridge and Australia, Sammy played several later in the season for Somerset 'with a fair amount of success' (30 wickets at 8.7). He also had his first match for the Gentlemen against the Players, and in September he played in his first Scarborough Festival. There he appeared against the Australians,

35

being chosen as a member of C.I. Thornton's XI. Sammy ran out of partners only a few runs short of victory.

There was more cricket that year, too, at club level. He was always happy to play for anyone, anywhere. Incredibly, on the Saturday before the Oval Test started on Monday he was enjoying himself in a country-house match in the Quantock Hills.

And so ended his first year in first-class cricket (apart from that single game in 1886). 'Although the season was a wet one, and all against my bowling, I enjoyed every moment of it, meeting all the great players of my time,' he reminisced. With one, Grace, he was to share many social hours off the field over the coming years.

One thing that impressed itself particularly on Sammy's memory was that 'I never saw in that season, as we see in the present time [the mid-1920s] anyone who was given out caught at the wicket or lbw stand and look as if he wasn't out. "Out" and out you go.' At the time he was writing this, he said, he sometimes read of batsmen being out lbw then knocking the stumps down and saying '*Now* I am out.' If such a thing had happened when he was captain, the offender 'would never have played in my side again.'

When *Wisden Cricketers' Almanack* appeared the following spring, there, under the heading 'Six Great Bowlers of the Year', appeared the name S.M.J. Woods. He was one of three Australians (the others being Ferris and Turner). His first-class record for the 1888 season was:

Overs	Maidens	Runs	Wickets	Average
930.2	342	1,711	117	14.73

Wisden recorded that Sammy 'bowls very fast right-hand, now and then sending in a good yorker' (it did not mention his well-concealed slower ball). 'He is a brilliant field at cover-point or extra mid-off, a sure catch, and a good punishing batsman with plenty of confidence.'

When he first appeared on the first-class scene, Sammy sometimes bowled a little wildly as he tried to give that extra bit of pace; a bit of a tearaway bowler at times, in fact. 'Very fast, but rather inclined to sacrifice pitch to pace' was how *Lillywhite's Cricketers' Annual* put it.

As he matured he still sent down occasional short-pitched deliveries and even, rarely, a beamer – the most dangerous kind, a flying full toss in the vicinity of the batsman's head. The short-pitched ball was likely to be deliberate: 'If the batsman gets above himself put one past his whiskers now and then', another Somerset bowler quoted him as saying; and he was also said to have recommended the use of a short-pitched delivery to unsettle a nervous batsman. At least once in a Gentlemen v. Players match Grace told him to 'Keep 'em short', and after hitting a batsman twice on the body as a result Sammy apologised to the man. A fellow countryman, Ernest Jones, who once brushed Grace's beard with a short delivery, called out: 'Sorry, Doctor, it slipped!'; but the terms of Sammy's apologies have not been recorded.

It has been alleged that his beamers, too, were sometimes deliberate, rather than the result of lack of control as he put every ounce of his great strength and energy into each delivery. Who can tell now? Yet if it had been thought that Sammy deliberately sent down such perilous balls, would he have earned and kept his great reputation for sportsmanship among his fellow cricketers and attracted so much affection?

Sir Pelham Warner, who regarded Sammy as 'a really great bowler' and the most intelligent fast man he ever faced, declared that he bowled at the wicket and not at the batsman, and if he did hit a man he apologised. C.B. Fry thought Sammy in his prime was 'one of the best fast bowlers of all time'; a complete artist, he said, with consummate skill in disguising his change of pace. And similar judgements came from other contemporaries.

Jessop once sat down and wrote his list of the fastest English bowlers. First (for sheer speed only) was Charles Kortright, of Essex; second (and the greatest fast bowler he ever encountered) was Surrey's Tom Richardson; third, Lancashire's Arthur Mold; and then fourth came Sammy. But by the time he faced Sammy, Jessop was told he was 'not quite as fast as he used to be'.

Perfect Partners

In the world of cricket there have been many famous duos – players who have complemented each other so well that they seem almost to have been made for each other. There have been few more perfect partners than Sammy and the brilliant wicket-keeper Gregor MacGregor, who stood right up to his fastest deliveries.

Moreover they shared rooms for a couple of years at Cambridge. One a boisterous extrovert, the other a Scot of dour aspect, they were partners, too, in many a prank, some of them foolhardy. Only an injury prevented their appearing on opposite sides in a Test match while still rooming together; and they did face each other on the international rugby field during this period. Later they were for years rival county cricket captains.

One of the sights that was ever to remain in the memories of those who watched Cambridge then was that of Sammy bowling and MacGregor keeping. Another member of the university team, Digby Jephson, later to captain Surrey, recalled:

> . . . I have never seen that machine-like precision – the foreshadowing of the possible – that existed between Gregor MacGregor and Sammy Woods. The faster Sam bowled, the nearer the sticks stood Mac, and he took the five-and-a-half ounces of leather, cork and string, as if it were a ping-pong ball! He took it on the off or the on-side with equal facility, and he would throw the ball back, time in and time out, with the suggestion that he was a little tired of the simplicity of it all.

Jephson played with MacGregor many times afterwards and whether it was a 'brown sherry' (country house) game or a first-class fixture, the keeper was 'always the same – even tempered – imperturbable – at times bordering on the cynical; rarely if ever depressed by fear of disaster, or over-elated with the joy of success.'

The Hon. R.H. Lyttleton declared that there was 'nothing so awe-

38

inspiring in cricket at the present day as to see Woods bowling on a hard wicket, and MacGregor standing up to the wicket with no long-stop.'

To the future 'Country Vicar', the pair were like demi-gods. On the rugby field they were 'each magnificent in his own position. MacGregor, broad-shouldered, dark and saturnine, cool, collected and unruffled at full-back: Sammy's towering form leading the forwards – always to the fore in every rush, and with a tackle that was deadly.'

And on the cricket field, he wrote, there was Sammy with a 'vigorous and determined run' up to the wicket, 'his pose as his arm swung over, like some all-powerful wheel: it was the embodiment of strength and virile grace'; while crouching behind the stumps MacGregor was 'quiet, unflurried, always safe', taking Sammy's expresses without a suspicion of flourish.

MacGregor, two years younger than Sammy, later played rugby for Scotland and for nine seasons captained Middlesex at cricket and played several times for England.

The two shared 'palatial rooms' at Prospect House, just opposite Jesus Common. Sammy remembered they 'always had a hot joint of beef on Sunday, which would be discussed by about half a dozen pals, and, of course, during the summer we had the amateurs of the visiting elevens to dine with us one evening of their matches'. Sammy went on:

> What times we had! Generally a dance and cards after dinner. I remember W.G. and Billy Murdoch bumping A.J.L. Hill and myself into the fireplace. I thought Hill was badly injured; the two former were just like a couple of boys – splendid boys those. I think we played all sorts of games, and all day and night, too, except when we two were reading, or rather one of us, and it wasn't me.

The 'boy' Grace was already in his forties. Hill, who appeared for Hampshire for many years, was to play Test cricket with Sammy in South Africa.

There are more stories (recorded by others) of the carousing at Prospect House. On one occasion, it was said, the two room-mates played 'bounce ball' with a diminutive college porter, who had interrupted a midnight revel. The episode came to an end when the unfortunate man became suspended by the waistband of his trousers, which had caught on a spike of the railings.

There were other incidents which also could have led to serious consequences. On the eve of a varsity match Sammy, in high spirits, knocked MacGregor against a plate-glass window and he went through it. One version said MacGregor was unhurt; another that he cut his hands but still kept wicket next morning. Sammy is said to have described the incident as the worst moment of his life.

Even in later years things could get dangerous with Sammy around. He and a younger Cambridge cricketer named Leonard Moon, who played for Middlesex and a few times for England, were invited to dine with MacGregor and Andrew Stoddart at the latter's digs in Hampstead. On arrival Sammy turned out the lights and chased the three Middlesex men round and round in the dark, over the furniture, while brandishing a carving knife.

Jephson remembered Sammy as being 'as rough as rough can be'. He recalled one incident when Sammy, a good billiards player, beat two hefty bookmakers in a Bristol hotel. One was unwise enough to say something to the other about 'billiards sharps'. Sammy heard, reacted violently, grabbing them each by the scruff of the neck and hammering their heads together until they fell dazed to the floor.

Sammy then rang for a waiter and asked for a syphon of soda. He sprayed the two inanimates, who slowly recovered. Sammy asked for the manager, and told the two bookmakers: 'Now here is the boss; ask him who I am,' and sauntered out.

Jephson also left an early glimpse of Sammy as a peremptory captain. Jephson had been fielding at mid-off for several overs, trying to cope with the hard hitting of Jack Lyons, an aggressive Australian batsman. The fielder then received curt instructions from his captain to field elsewhere: 'Come on, you little blighter, out of it!' and Sammy took his place.

Although Sammy could be 'as rough as rough can be', Jephson said, 'yet he was gentle as a child, for he grasped the stick of life at both ends.' He had 'a strong lovable personality'. But while slow to wrath he was, when roused, 'a perfect tornado'. Gilbert Jessop, another who knew him well, said there was nothing vindictive in Sammy's character, 'but you are such a big beggar that you don't know your own strength'. Really, said Jessop, he was of a very gentle disposition.

The weather was not to save Oxford in the second varsity match. With Sammy proving almost unplayable they were beaten by an innings and 105 runs. From the first ball, a full toss, he took a return catch, and ended the innings with 6 for 42 in 20.4 overs (this was the first year of the five-ball over). In reply to Cambridge's 300, Oxford could not reach 90 in their second innings, Sammy claiming another five wickets.

Although only 22 Sammy was already nearing his peak as a bowler. Twice more that season he took 11 wickets in a match – against Yorkshire and for the Gentlemen of England against I Zingari at Scarborough. He was the country's leading amateur wicket-taker, with 74 victims at 16.55 runs apiece. There were also a few matches for Somerset late in the season.

Sammy's standing in the game was already regarded by the editor of *Wisden*, Charles Pardon, as sufficient for him to be numbered among prominent cricketers whose views were sought on various questions of the day for the 1890 edition. Sammy replied that he approved the five-ball over and also the new law allowing captains to declare at any time on the third day of a match. He also favoured a suggestion that in drawn games a committee of sporting journalists should adjudicate and awarded the match either half to each side or three-quarters to one and a quarter to the other. It was not an idea, though, that found much support elsewhere.

The following year Sammy captained Cambridge, a very strong side with the newcomers including F. Stanley Jackson, a future England captain. Sammy had spotted a great all-rounder in the making when he saw Jackson playing in the Eton v Harrow match the previous year. He was quick to give a diffident Jackson his Blue.

Lord Hawke, the Yorkshire captain, recorded Jackson's own story of how this happened. Yorkshire were playing Cambridge, a match which Hawke's men only narrowly won and in which Sammy took 11 for 131 on a perfect pitch. At one point when Cambridge were batting Sammy asked Jackson why he was looking so glum.

Jackson: 'Well, I've got to go in next wicket, and the bowling's pretty beastly.'

Sammy: 'Take my advice and don't behave like a baby. You can have your Blue now, if you like.'

There were three other future Test players in the side against Oxford: MacGregor, Francis Ford (already playing for Middlesex), and Arthur Hill (later to play for Hampshire). There was also a future England batsman in the Oxford team: Lionel Palairet, Sammy's Somerset team-mate.

In a low-scoring, rain-affected match, with only a day and a half of play possible, Cambridge won by seven wickets, the scores being: Oxford 42 and 108, Cambridge 97 and 54 for 7. Sammy's figures were 4 for 25 and 4 for 31.

His countrymen were back again. Sammy briefly recorded: 'I was to have assisted the Australians v England, but had injuries.' Had he been able to play he would have been trying to bowl out his room-mate. For MacGregor's talent had been noticed, too, and he played for England in both Tests that summer (the third was abandoned).

It was still, however, a memorable season again for Sammy. His outstanding performance came early, in the first of Cambridge's important matches, the fixture against C.I. Thornton's England XI. He took all 10 wickets in the second innings (in spite of his famous hot lobster breakfast), after having taken five in the first.

The side Thornton took to Cambridge on May 12–13 was a strong one – mostly Kent and Middlesex amateurs, but with four professionals. Five of the side were past, present, or future Test players. It was a low-scoring match (Cambridge may have had Sammy, but Thornton could call on two great Lancashire bowlers, Mold and Johnny Briggs). The Cambridge men, thanks almost entirely to Sammy and his room-mate, won by four wickets.

Cambridge had long been regarded for their entertainment of visiting sides and Sammy, now the host captain, needed no bidding to carry on the tradition. Thornton and the other amateurs were invited to breakfast on the second day. They included Henry Forster (Oxford and Hampshire), later as Lord Forster a Governor of Australia who was to take a special interest in cricket in the Commonwealth and entertain visiting England teams.

In front of the guests on the table was a large dish of hot lobsters, with plenty of Jesus audit ale to wash them down. There was also a sufficiency of bacon and eggs and cold tongue. When Thornton saw the spread he said: 'Good Lord, we can't eat hot lobsters for breakfast!' Sammy replied: 'Well, I'm sorry, but if you can't you will have to do without fish this morning.' One of the guests did try a lobster, but the rest stuck to the bacon and eggs and tongue. Sammy and MacGregor, however, piled into the lobsters and had their fill of beer.

The story as usually told is that thus fortified Sammy ran through the ten second-innings wickets. The truth is different, but no less remarkable.

On the first day Thornton's men had tumbled out for 68, with Sammy claiming half the wickets for 19 runs. MacGregor, who took five catches in the match, top-scored with 36 when Cambridge replied that afternoon with 130. Going in again in the late afternoon the visitors faced Sammy at his most venomous, and when stumps were drawn he had bowled five and had a sixth caught by MacGregor. There were only 29 runs on the board.

There were, thus, only four wickets left when play resumed next day after the lobsters. Sammy quickly took one of them, but then the Middlesex captain, A.J. Webbe, and another Middlesex man, P.J. de Paravicini, made a stand of 63 which gave the game new interest. Perhaps the lobsters were laying heavily on Sammy's stomach. At one point, unable to break the partnership, he thought of taking himself off, and asked MacGregor: 'Who shall I put on here?' MacGregor, who was rated by Sammy as 'a great judge of the game', replied: 'Keep on yourself if you want to win.' Sammy took the advice and went on to get the remaining wickets and dismiss their opponents for 133. He ended with the figures:

Overs	Maidens	Runs	Wickets
31	6	69	10

Seven of the ten were bowled, the others caught, one by Sammy himself. At the other end two future Surrey bowlers, Jephson and Edward Streatfield (who had taken five wickets in the first innings) toiled in vain. Sammy's figures for the match were 15 wickets for 88 runs off 249 deliveries.

Fortified by a lunch-time drink, Sammy produced another memorable match-winning performance that summer. He played under his room-mate in the Jesus College XI fixtures, and MacGregor led the college to victory in 15 of 16 games (the other was drawn). The most startling result came in that against the Magpies, virtually the pick of the rest of Cambridge. With nine wickets left, 20 runs to get, and an afternoon's play still ahead, the Magpies looked certain of victory. Sammy remembered: 'I had a small bottle of "fizz" and then took 8 wickets for three runs, and we won.'

It was on Jesus Close that Sammy once hit 11 runs off one ball. It went into the far corner of the field and the fielder, thinking it was a certain boundary, did not chase it soon enough.

Just before the Oval Test in August the room-mates were together playing against the Australians for a Cambridge Past and Present XI at Leyton. It ended in a draw, the tourists not playing their strongest side. Unfortunately Sammy strained himself and in the second innings bowled lobs. For once MacGregor let him down. *Wisden* recorded that he had never kept wicket so indifferently. Perhaps he was thinking of the next match. At any rate he fumbled stumping chances off Sammy's lobs that he would probably not have missed once in 20 times.

Sammy played against the Australians no fewer than three times that summer, although he bowled little due to strains. In June he had led Cambridge University in a drawn match against the tourists, and then in early September he featured in what *Cricket* called 'one of the most exciting finishes of the season'. He and MacGregor were included in Lord Londesborough's XI, a very strong side, almost an England XI.

On a rain-affected wicket at Scarborough the Australians were dismissed for 77, but then the England team were bowled out for 39. Turner, the Australian 'Terror', was at his best in conditions ideal for him, and was almost unplayable. Sammy once described Turner as 'the most dangerous bowler in the game'. It was perhaps in this innings that he experienced an over which he was never to forget, being hit in succession on the funny bone, inside the right knee, stunned by a rising ball on the chin, and then hit on the belt buckle.

In the second innings Australia were all out for 60, leaving Lord Londesborough's men to get 99 to win. At 66 for 9 it looked all over, but then the last pair, Sammy and MacGregor, nearly pulled it off with some plucky batting, only for MacGregor to go lbw with the total on 90.

There were also one or two matches for Somerset, then challenging for a place among the first-class counties. The county had discovered Sammy in Norfolk 'having a rest' for a week or two on the Broads. His 'rest' there included more cricket, and he hit a couple of centuries. Somerset asked him to play in their fixture at Leicester in early August. Sammy tells a story against himself of what happened there.

William Roe, who was captaining the county for this match, won the toss and decided to bat. He pondered on who was to open, and Sammy, 'never being bashful', as he himself put it, said: 'I am in pretty good form. Who's coming in with me?' Now Leicester had two formidable pace men, both professionals, in Arthur Woodcock, who was very fast, and Dick Pougher. Sammy related: 'I was missed first ball at slip by Woodcock off Pougher, and out off Woodcock's first ball, caught by Pougher.'

When Leicester batted Sammy was, he admitted, 'very erratic' on a fiery pitch. He claimed the first three wickets, all played on, in a few minutes, 'amid a lot of comments from the crowd'. The way he was using the ball, it may be taken, was not to their liking. The score was then 33 for 3, and 29 of the runs had come off Sammy. 'Still, we won,' he added. Altogether he took nine wickets in the match, and Leicester lost by ten wickets.

In his final summer, that of 1891, two matches stood out among Cambridge's triumphs. MacGregor was now captain – 'the best I ever played under', said Sammy. It was again the Australian's bowling that won the day.

The first was the defeat of the county champions, Surrey, at the Oval on June 11 and 12. Surrey fielded the team that took part in most of their fixtures that season. Bowling unchanged in both innings from the gasworks end, and helped by the wicket, Sammy took 14 wickets for 154 runs: seven in each innings, nine of them bowled. The promising youngster whom Sammy had spotted and given his Blue, Stanley Jackson, top scored with 62 and Cambridge were victors by 19 runs.

Jephson, who was in the winning team, recalled the occasion as a rare one when MacGregor's usual tranquillity broke down. He said in his quiet way: 'Let 'em go, Sam.' And, for almost the first time, the wicketkeeper stood back. Sammy, in the right mood and with the wicket suiting him, 'let 'em go'. Some of the champion county's batsmen edged towards the square-leg umpire as Sammy delivered and the stumps, unguarded, were lifted from the ground several times. It was Sammy at his very best. Surrey, needing 122 to win, were all out for 103.

Jephson recalled: 'As we walked back to the pavilion a faint, very faint smile illuminated for a moment the dark features of MacGregor. "Well bowled, Sam" was all he said.'

Just over a fortnight later MacGregor led Cambridge to a dramatic victory in the varsity match – the closest result in the four in which Sammy played. Cambridge batted first, and in the first hour their new captain made a generous gesture which Sammy doubtless applauded when he allowed Oxford to replace in the team a player who had been injured fielding. In reply to Cambridge's 210 Oxford were dismissed for 108, Sammy taking 7 for 60. Being required to follow on it looked as if they faced a heavy defeat.

Wilson, Sammy's fellow Australian at Brighton College, then turned the tide. In the first innings Sammy had dismissed him for a duck, deceiving him with his slower ball. In the second Wilson survived an appeal first ball, and then went on to score 53. It was the only half-century any Oxford batsman scored in a varsity match when Sammy was bowling. Oxford totalled 191, and MacGregor's men needed only 90. But there was an unexpected collapse, partly due to the poor light. The scores were level when MacGregor was bowled and only two wickets remained. Sportingly MacGregor had not appealed against the light, although it had become quite dark and there was no screen at the pavilion end.

Sammy had not expected to bat. He was always quick to the wicket, and on this occasion he did not wait to put on his pads and gloves. He picked up someone else's bat and *ran* to the wicket. Facing George Berkeley, a left-arm medium-pacer whose figures at this point were 5 for 16, Sammy disdained to take guard. He had been loudly cheered to the wicket by the Cambridge men in the crowd. Now there was silence. To the first ball he advanced down the wicket and hit it with one bounce to the long-on boundary. He ran back to the pavilion for what must rank as perhaps the quicket scoring innings, from gate to gate, that Lord's has seen. It was a *Boy's Own Paper* ending to his last varsity match.

In the four encounters between the universities Sammy bowled 878 deliveries and took 36 wickets for 318 runs, an average cost of 8.83. In all his 28 first-class matches for Cambridge, his bowling record was:

Wickets	Runs	Average	5 wickets in innings	10 wickets in match
190	2,838	14.93	19	7

And with the bat:

Innings	Not out	Runs	Highest score	Average
48	9	837	79 not out	20.92

Figures never tell the whole story, and Sammy was no great believer in averages and league tables. But his record places him among the very best of all Oxbridge bowlers.

Sammy left, needless to say, without a degree. There were some who felt he deserved an honorary award, and it was once suggested that Oxford, who had suffered at his hands, should make him an M.A.

for his sporting achievements. Professor Thomas Case, president of Corpus Christi College, played for Oxford before Sammy was born and through his long life was prominent in the affairs of the Oxford University Cricket Club. He much admired Sammy and was said to have suggested the honour. He may not have been joking, either.

Somerset and America

S omerset, one of the loveliest of English counties, is a land of contrasts and surprises. There are peaceful green hills and fertile vales, moors where red deer roam and the Doones once rode, busy seaside towns and remote picture-postcard villages, caves where prehistoric man lived, and the Levels with their traces of the lake dwellers and haunted by legends of King Alfred and King Arthur. Somerset's surprises include, for the uninitiated, its cider and its cricket.

This is not, judged merely on its championship record, one of the foremost cricketing counties, but for unpredictability, for entertainment, and for the fervour of its supporters it challenges the rest. It took almost a century for Somerset to win its first title (in the one-day competitions – it has yet to win the county championship). Yet many times while low in the table it has inflicted unexpected and sometimes humiliating defeats on high-riding counties, as Yorkshiremen will know.

Sammy Woods is remembered affectionately in his adopted county for his role in these giant-killing acts; as well as (among many other things) for being one of the small band who helped Somerset to achieve first-class status in 1891. He then became for years a mainstay of the team and, for longer than anyone else, its captain.

For a few brief years he was one of the most feared bowlers in the land. Then, as he burnt himself out as a bowler, he developed into a formidable batsman; while all the time being one of the game's outstanding fielders. He was, as Grace said, a giant in stature. He stood 6ft 1in, weighed 13 stone 6 lb., and was enormously strong. In the *Jubilee Book of Cricket*, K.S. Ranjitsinhji also called him 'a giant' and wrote: 'He seems big and strong in his clothes, but when stripped, his physique is even more striking. The power in his huge thighs, long back, and knotted shoulders is immense.' He presented an awesome sight as he ran in to deliver a lightning ball, arm high over his shoulder. 'On any wicket he was a dangerous opponent,' said Grace.

Sammy was careless and casual in his attire. There was enough slack in his flannel trousers to sail a Bridgwater coastal 'clipper', as someone put it. The sleeves of his linen shirt defied control, one or the other always flopping about his wrists, and the tail of his shirt often came out of his trousers. But there was nothing casual about the cricket: he was always in a hurry to get to the wicket, not least in a crisis. Warner said, 'That determined chin of his used to look more determined than ever when he came out to bat to set right the failure of half his side.'

There was never any difficulty in picking Sammy out in the field, however far off he was: he was the one without a hat. His shock of corn-coloured hair led Grace among others to call him 'Shockhead'. Although in team photographs he often wore a cap, it came off in a match. 'I never wear a cap, and feel sure it would make a difference to me in some way if I did,' he once said in an interview when discussing superstitions. In fact, there is a record of him once wearing one on a very hot day in 1892, just as a 'precaution' after another player had suffered a touch of sunstroke. And perhaps in South Africa or the West Indies he must have done so sometimes. One feels that if he were playing today he would have scorned the use of a helmet. On the rugby field, however, he always wore a cap, to prevent his getting 'footballer's ear'.

After his debut for Somerset in 1886 Sammy played a handful of games for the county each season while still at Cambridge, mostly towards the end of the summer. He was the county's leading wicket-taker in 1887, and but for that missed catch would have had Grace out first ball when Somerset played Gloucester, who were already a first-class county. In four games for Somerset in 1888 he took 31 wickets (all but seven of them bowled). He headed the county's bowling averages that year and again the following season. His brother Harris played in a couple of games for Somerset, too, and like Sammy also represented the county at rugby and soccer.

Sammy's most notable achievement for the county in the summer of 1889 was to take 12 for 54 at Lord's and be chiefly responsible for inflicting a decisive defeat within a day on M.C.C. and Ground.

It was in large part due to the bowling of Sammy and a couple of professionals Somerset managed to find the money to employ – Ted Tyler, a slow left-arm bowler, and George Nichols, fast-medium – that by the end of the decade they were the outstanding second-class county. After 1890 their bid to join the eight first-class counties – Gloucester, Kent, Lancashire, Middlesex, Nottingham, Surrey, Sussex, and Yorkshire – could no longer be denied. The other counties would have to wait a bit more.

Led now by Herbert Hewett – an Oxford man, a lawyer, and nicknamed 'The Colonel' – Somerset that season won all their first 10 matches (five times by an innings). Apart from their bowling strength, they had in Hewett and the 20-year-old Oxford Blue Lionel Palairet a formidable pair of opening batsmen. Then, in a dramatic climax to the season, they tied the final match. Sammy, one of its heroes, had until then played little for the county that season, being much engaged elsewhere and also suffering from strains. Regrettably, too, he failed to turn out for them at Birmingham, despite having said (according to a newspaper) that he would. No reason was given. He made up for it, though, in this last match.

The visitors to Taunton were Middlesex. Earlier in the season at Lord's Somerset had surprisingly beaten their first-class opponents. On that occasion Sammy had been only a bystander, having a severe strain to his side. The return match was eagerly looked forward to, and Middlesex were determined on their revenge.

The ground had been affected by heavy rain, and it was a bowlers' game. Somerset scored 107 and 127 and Middlesex, after making 108, needed 127 for victory. Their captain, Webbe, seemed to have set them on the way to victory. There were loud cheers round the ground, therefore, when on 57 he was given out caught behind off Sammy, who had been brought back on to bowl. Still, Middlesex hopes were still very high: they needed only 13 for victory with five wickets in hand.

Then came a collapse, with Sammy and Nichols sharing the honours. With two runs needed, Sammy caught and bowled the No. 10, and in came the last man, Maurice Dauglish. He hit Sammy to leg, ran one and then tried the second, only to be run out feet short of the wicket.

The *County Gazette*'s man at the match wrote:

> The match thus ended in a tie. There was tremendous excitement and the spectators, rushing on to the field, sur-rounded the players as they retired to the pavilion and cheered again and again, Nichols and Woods being special favourites. Hats were thrown in the air and the ladies in the gallery waved handkerchiefs and heartily joined in the enthusiasm. Such a scene has never been witnessed on the ground before.

Sammy had taken 5 for 61 in that second innings, giving him a match aggregate of 9 for 95, but Tyler, who took eight, and Nichols were equal heroes, as Sammy acknowledged.

At the end of the season the Mayor gave a banquet to the team at the Castle Hotel, the town's premier hotel, attended by councillors and leading local supporters, a company of nearly 100 in all. It was a magnificent occasion. The *County Gazette* was there, of course, and described the setting:

> Depending from the framework of the partition which usually divides the saloon into two rooms were richly-coloured Indian palamores arranged in graceful folds and festoons, underneath which were several cleverly-designed trophies, consisting of bats, wickets, balls, pads and other cricket materials set off with the County Club and town colours. The table was decorated with much elegance and taste. Along the whole length ran a line of liberty art silk in old gold, relieved by tracery of ivy tendrils, and the table was lit by about 20 very handsome electric lamps of the newest designs, with vari-coloured shades to subdue the brilliant of the electric light. These lamps served also the purpose of flower and fruit stands, and imparted an effect to the table as rich as it was original.

The menu included turbot, oyster cutlets, beef, lamb, goslings, chicken, venison, and grouse.

There were, of course, speeches, including one by Sammy, the report of which was frequently punctuated by: (Laughter). There was a dig at Lord's delay in admitting Somerset as a first-class county. He didn't believe in this tomfoolery (said Sammy) about going on till 1893 to grow into a first-class county (Hear, Hear). There was also a reference to that vital Middlesex wicket, the dismissal of Webbe. The Middlesex captain did not believe he was out, and it was Sammy and not the wicketkeeper, the Rev. A.P. Wickham, who had appealed. The *Gazette*, continuing its report, quoted Sammy: 'They could always trust him [Wickham] to catch a man out at the wicket when they wanted to win the match (Laughter). He would say no more about that (Laughter) but they must remember that the umpire's decision was final.

Wickham, too, one suspects, was not sure that Webbe had touched the ball; but Sammy was always a strong believer in accepting the

51

umpire's decision whether, as in this case, it was in his favour or whether it was not.

In his speech Sammy paid tribute to the two professionals, Nichols and Tyler, who shared the burden of the Somerset bowling with him for several years. The admiration was probably mutual, for generally in those days it was the professionals who did all the hard work bowling. Amateurs who put as much effort as Sammy into their bowling, and kept at it for long spells, were rare.

Not being well paid, the professionals supplemented their cricket earnings in other ways. Tyler (later to play alongside Sammy in a Test) had several business ventures, including a sports shop in partnership with Nichols. An advertisement includes this undated testimonial signed by S.M.J. Woods, of Jesus College, Cambridge:

> Gentlemen – I write to thank you for the splendid bats I bought from you last season. One was a very fine one, with which I scored 1,400 runs. You might retain two or three for me to look at when I next come down to Somerset. Hope you will be in form this season.

Somerset's first season in first-class cricket was Sammy's last at Cambridge, and he ended it as the country's leading amateur wicket-taker, with 134 victims costing just under 17 apiece. This was nearly twice as many wickets as his nearest rival, his countryman Ferris, and more than all but four of the professional bowlers. He headed not only the Cambridge but the Somerset averages. For the county in 11 matches he took 72 wickets at 17.4.

After ups and downs Somerset could feel well satisfied with their first-class debut, winning five and drawing one of their 12 fixtures. Sammy took 11 wickets and, coming in at a critical moment, hit a half-century in their win over Yorkshire at Bradford (he had also figured prominently in Cambridge's win over the same county that May). Sammy recalled:

> At luncheon time I was walking about when an old gentle-man came up to me and said, 'Here, lad, thou'st played fine cricket; here's a knife for thee.' There were about 30 different instruments in it. I only required two in any knife I use, a blade and a corkscrew, so I gave it to a gamekeeper.

But the sensational match of the season, the one that really put Somerset on the first-class map, was the newcomers' defeat of the county champions. In June, while still at Cambridge, Sammy had taken 14 wickets in the university's surprise win over Surrey. Now he was again the hero, with an amusing tale to tell of how he took the final wicket to win the day.

Earlier, at the Oval, a match Sammy missed through injury, Somerset had been thoroughly routed by Surrey, being dismissed for the same total, 37, in each innings, and losing by an innings and 375 runs. Now, on their home ground and at full strength, they went out for revenge. Surrey batted last, needing 372 in just under five hours. The visitors decided to settle for a draw, and with only half an hour left still had five wickets left.

But Sammy and Co. had not given up hope of winning, and suddenly wickets began to fall. The ninth man was out with less than ten minutes to go. No 11, John Sharpe, joined fellow professional Harry Wood, the wicketkeeper. Not only did they defy the bowlers but Sharpe took four runs off Sammy.

It was the last over, Sharpe facing Sammy. The first ball was wild and flew over the batsman's head. The second was little better. There is more than one version of the third. One is that those first two deliveries had so unsettled the batsman that he backed away from the next, which was of perfect accuracy. But Sammy's own version is one to treasure.

According to him, as he was walking back to his bowling mark, the non-striker, Wood, said: 'Keeps his end up well for a man with one eye, eh?' Then (Sammy wrote): 'I said, "Which one?" "Left one." I bowled my first round-arm ball of my life, and hit his off-stump. Had I not had the information we wouldn't have won.'

Another version makes it the middle stump. And there are differences as to whether it was a full toss, or as Sammy averred (writing long after), a long hop! The essential thing was that the score sheet read: Sharpe b Woods 4; and Sammy's ninth wicket of the match resulted in victory by 130 runs.

Sammy felt that this win 'made Somerset cricket'. The spectators 'went barmy, flung their hats in the air, and hit each other about'. It was talked about long after.

Not for the only time over the years Sammy's deeds were recorded at length in verse. The author was Alfred Perceval Graves, father of Robert Graves, the poet and writer, and himself a minor literary figure. 'Father O'Flynn', which appeared in one of his many books, became one of the best-known songs of the late Victorian era. Graves, then working in Somerset as inspector of schools, was very keen on cricket and saw the match. He at once wrote 'Zummerzet v Zurrey', a narrative of over 130 lines in Somerset dialect, and it was quickly in print. Part of it reads:

Then zeconds zimed like minutes, and minutes weary hours,
As Sharpe and Wood again wi'stood our bowlers' desperate
    powers.
Vive – vour – dree minutes now were left; they
    vielders vlyin' pass
At every maiden over's end, like swallows o'er the grass.
Two minutes – one – vrom Zammy's arm a zudden yorker
    zails,
And passes Sharpe, and like a shell explodes upon his bails.
Then we went wild! Tha straain wur such, the pipple
    bust the barriers,
And went vor tha pavilion like a pack of huntin' harriers;
And one oald gent his hat a-sent into the river zaailin',
Another like a coalt he jomps all vours across the paailin'.
And a fat old bloke went nigh to choake tell his buttons
    I undunned,
And then a blubbered like a babe vor joy that we'd a-wunned.

The verses conclude:

Well, o' course we cheered vor Zummerzet as long as we
    could cheer,
And we hed out zplendid Zammy, our bowler wi'out peer,
And our clever Cap'm Hewett and our clinkin' pair of pros,
Not forgettin' a good ringin' cheer vor our gallant Zurrey foes.

A quarter of a century later Graves' daughter, Susan, was matron of an Army convalescent hospital in Alexandria where 'Zammy' arrived as a patient. He told her he always carried a copy of the verses with him.

Sammy had now reached a crossroads. He had come to the end of what *Wisden* called his 'brilliant career' at Cambridge, alluding to his sporting rather than his academic accomplishments. There is little doubt that he was considering returning to Australia. Perhaps his father felt that enough money had been spent on making him into a gentleman, and that it was time to come home and take up a business career; a prospect which one imagines held little attraction for Sammy.

A former English captain, Allan Steel, wrote at the time:

> What a pity we cannot keep this fine young cricketer at home; we could do very well with him in Gentlemen v Players matches for the next five or six years. We are told that Ferris has taken a house or cottage of some sort near Bristol in order to secure some so-called qualification for Gloucester . . . I should like to hear Woods had done the same thing in any English city he pleased.

However *Wisden* reported that at the end of his time at Cambridge 'it was feared that Mr Woods would be lost to Somersetshire after the past season, but happily his return to Australia has been delayed for at least another year.' Although he did not take Steel's advice to take a house in an English city, he was beginning to put down roots at Bridgwater, albeit never more than in a rented room or two.

Perhaps it was an invitation by Lord Hawke to join him on a short tour of North America that autumn of 1891, and the fact that he was by now a regular choice for the England rugby XV, that helped Sammy to decide to stay on – at least for the present. The letters passing between him and his family in Manly, New South Wales, would make interesting reading if they had survived. John Woods was, after all, still providing the wherewithal for his son's pleasant existence as a sporting gentleman. Sammy was no great letter writer, but his father must have been persuaded somehow to continue with the remittance for a while longer. Perhaps he was a bit disappointed at his son's lack of academic qualifications; but, after all, Sammy had become a national celebrity in the field of sport.

Lord Hawke, the illustrious Yorkshire captain, picked his men carefully for the private tours he arranged and which did so much to spread the love of cricket in other lands. In North America, cricket had been an established game before the Civil War, and indeed the first overseas tour by any English cricketers was to that continent in 1859. One result of the Civil War, however, was that baseball quickly became the national game: cricket equipment was hard to come by during the years of fighting and the maintenance and marking of pitches for the English game was more difficult. Countless soldiers learned baseball during the war and when it was over they did not go back to cricket. But it still remained a popular game for some. In Philadelphia in particular it reached a standard as high as in many English counties.

The party of 12 which sailed from Liverpool in the *City of New York* on September 15 was made up almost entirely of former Oxford and Cambridge men; all amateurs, of course. Apart from Lord Hawke and Sammy there were three others who had played first-class cricket regularly in the past season. There were Hewett, who was a gifted left-hand opening bat; Kingsmill Key, later to captain Surrey, who had been on an earlier tour; and 'Chawles' Wright, of Nottingham, opening bat and wicketkeeper, later a Test player. Wright's serious cricket was unfortunately to end a little prematurely when he lost an eye in an accident while shooting partridges.

The rest of the party had mainly played no more than an occasional county match, and were probably chosen as much for social reasons and for their qualities as good ambassadors. They included a future earl, Lord Throwley, and his brother, the Hon. Henry Milles, who had both briefly played for Kent. The most talented of these others, Charles Wreford-Brown, who had a few games for Gloucester, is better remembered as a soccer player, and is said to have been the first to use the word 'soccer' for association football.

Sammy was not in the original list drawn up by Hawke, but was persuaded to join the party in place of another young Somerset player, Lionel Palairet, a stylish opening batsman who could not get away from Oxford that autumn. Sammy's inclusion much strengthened the bowling, and batting too, and he was without doubt the hero of the tour.

The voyage was at times a rough one, and at least one of the party (but not Sammy) was very seasick. The two most important of the eight matches played in a month were the first, both against the Gentlemen of Philadelphia on the fine Germanstown ground. A splendid permanent grandstand had been erected in time for the visit. The first match was on September 25–27, the second on October 1–2. Sammy recorded:

> We played the Philadelphians the day after we landed, and were beaten by eight wickets. We had hardly found our land legs. Lord Hawke had quite a lot of letters to answer after our defeat, praying us for the Lord's sake to beat them in the return game.

Thousands of Americans let out a yell as victory came in that first encounter. From the grandstand hundreds of parasols and handkerchiefs were waved, from the crowd by the ropes hats and canes were thrown in the air, and from the coaches camped round the field came the tooting of horns. In the midst of all this, the band struck up the 'Star Spangled Banner'. It was, a newspaper reported, 'certainly the most noteworthy game of cricket that ever took place on this continent'.

Sammy had bowled badly, his four wickets being expensive; and *Wisden* said the Englishmen's defeat was 'in a great measure' attributable to his performance. Equally, the tourists' revenge in the second match was largely due to Sammy finding his land legs. He took 15 for 86, and the home gentlemen lost by four wickets. A third match was suggested, but the tight schedule made this impossible.

The rest of the programme was more enjoyable from the social point of view than for the cricket. The opposition was somewhat less formidable than in Philadelphia. In the third match, against a New York 16, time ran out with the home side facing defeat. Sammy hit 92 in opening the batting, and took 10 of the 15 wickets in the New Yorkers' first innings. He brought back with him an account of the match in an American newspaper, part of which reads:

> The next to take strike was the home captain (he had been in the Rugby School XI and wore a light blue cap and sash). A Symphony in Blue. He walked out very slowly to the crease and looked about. Meanwhile the Demon Woods – he looks like a Yorkshire farmer [why Yorkshire, I thought most farmers looked alike, wondered Sammy] – had his eagle eye on him. Woods ran up to the sticks, swinging his arm round his head like the kick of a Georgian mule. There was a crash in the timber yard, and the Symphony in Blue went back to the club-house a wiser and sadder man.

Sammy ran out two colleagues when the visitors batted, and when his county captain, Hewett, arrived at the wicket, he said: 'Now then, Shockhead, I suppose I am the next.' Instead Sammy ran himself out, just short of a century.

The other matches, mostly won with ease by an innings, were in Baltimore, Boston (where Sammy took 13 for 25), Chicago, Toronto, and Ottawa. In all he took 76 wickets (more than the rest of the bowlers together) for 7 runs apiece.

In Ontario Sammy performed the hat-trick, and was presented with a white hat suitably inscribed, which he took back with him to England.

The cricket had its lighter moments. In Boston Sammy was bowling to someone he termed an 'old gentleman' and gave him 'some very easy balls indeed', enabling him to hit 17 and outscore his partner. Unfortunately, not being content with this, the prolific batsman could not resist telling his team-mates that 'anybody could hit Woods'. He promised to really show them in the second innings.

The team got fed up with this and asked Sammy to bowl to him as he did to the rest of them. Sammy 'hardly liked doing it', but decided that a fast yorker would not hurt the 'old gentleman' and could settle the matter quickly. It did, and Sammy's figures in this innings were 7 for 7.

Another of Sammy's anecdotes was about a match in Chicago when Wright was bowled first ball. He restored the bails and told the bowler it was a good 'un for a trial ball. However, it didn't come off, and he had to retire to the pavilion.

The tour began in tropical weather (one member of the party, George Hillyard, of Middlesex and later Leicester, suffered sunstroke and had to return home early), and ended in snow in Ontario. The cricket, other than in Philadelphia, was mostly one-sided, and many of the memories the team took home were rather of the social side of the tour. The hospitality showered on them was wonderful wherever they went. There were reception committees always – generally dressed in frock coats and tall hats, and christened by Hewett 'the pallbearers'. Visits arranged for them ranged from baseball and racing to a stud farm; and, of course, Niagara Falls. On the debit side, there was a lot of tedious travel.

At a dance held in their honour in Philadelphia over 500 packed into a room that could hold little more than half that number comfortably. Sammy was fond of dancing, but at that time could not get on too well with the craze of the couple keeping their hands away from the body and using a motion 'as if using a pump-handle', as he put it. He inadvertently gave one partner a black eye, and his comments, including 'This is worse than football', caused much amusement when they appeared in the newspapers next day. 'How my lady friends chaff me,' he said. And he found the ladies of Philadelphia, Baltimore, and Boston 'charming' (and, one hopes, those of New York and Chicago and the Canadian cities).

Eight matches in a month, and the party was back in England on

November 5, in time for the rugby season and, in Sammy's case, more internationals.

In his cricket, Sammy was probably now at the peak of his bowling. In the 1892 season he took over 150 wickets. He also scored his first first-class century, and it came against his old university. He hit the runs before lunch, as he did in two other of his 19 first-class hundreds.

The match was Somerset's first visit to Fenner's. As it turned out the visitors had to be recorded not as Somerset but as 'H.W. Hewett's Team'. Hewett had been unable to produce more than 10 players, and it was agreed eventually that he could borrow not one but two Cambridge men (MacGregor one of them) who were not qualified for Somerset, and that it would be a 12-a-side match. It proved an easy win for the visitors.

Sammy was let off behind the wicket when he was on 12, and his appetite for quick running nearly led to his running himself and his partner out once or twice. He was caught in the slips off Jackson when he had hit 103, including 13 fours.

Sammy's 1892 haul of first-class wickets was 153, the biggest of his career, at an average cost of 16.13. Only two other amateurs claimed more than 50, Jackson and Ferris each taking 80. Although most of the hard work of bowling was done by the professionals, only one of these, Middlesex's Jack Hearne, dismissed more batsmen than Sammy: 163 at just under 16 apiece. There can be no doubt that but for a strain which severely curtailed Sammy's bowling in the last five county matches he would have passed Hearne's total.

Altogether that season Sammy bowled 1,055 overs in 25 first-class matches – a punishing total for even a medium-pacer, and he was still rather more than that. They were, of course, still five-ball overs, and were the equivalent of 879 of today's six-ball overs. Few of even the most-used slow bowlers of today would expect to bowl so much in first-class games in a season.

A few days into September the strain which Sammy had suffered in mid-August in a match against Nottingham had gone, and he was back in full flow when he played for the West of England against a strong East of England XI at Portsmouth. He took 13 wickets for 109 runs. In the next match, for the Gentlemen v the Players at Hastings, he took 11 wickets. It was the fifth time that season he had claimed 10 or more victims in a match, the other occasions being against Middlesex, Kent, and Oxford University.

In the Portsmouth match Sammy hit the stumps nine times. Through that remarkable season he needed no help from fielders or wicketkeeper in despatching almost two-thirds of his victims. Of the 153, he bowled 83, caught and bowled 11, and had one lbw.

It was a good year for Somerset, who won eight of their 16 county matches and finished third of the nine first-class counties. Only rain prevented them doing the double over Yorkshire in a match at Taunton in which Hewett and Lionel Palairet scored 346 in just over three and a half hours for the first wicket – 'as lovely batting as I ever wish to see,' said Sammy.

The following season, 1893, was to prove a turning point in his career. There was the curious and controversial matter of the Australian match at Taunton which was to result in Sammy taking over as county captain. And there was the falling off in his bowling, which was soon noticeably losing its sting. He dropped to fourth in the Somerset averages, his 59 wickets costing nearly 25 runs apiece; and the county finished one off the bottom of the table. Supporters fervently hoped it was just a temporary decline in Sammy's bowling but, apart from occasional glimpses of his old self, he was never again quite the same terror to batsmen. Soon it was his batting that was to be more important.

The arrival of the Australians towards the end of July (their first visit to Taunton for over a decade) was looked forward to by thousands of cricket fans in Somerset and beyond. Many travelled for hours to get to the county ground only to find, alas, that although it was now bright and sunny the ground was saturated from earlier rain. Only members were admitted during the morning, and at 11 o'clock the umpires inspected the pitch and ruled that there would be no play that day. The huge crowd waiting outside was not at all happy. There were groans and jeers as the Australians packed picnic baskets at their nearby hotel, hired a large horse-brake, and went off to enjoy themselves five or six miles away in the Quantock Hills.

The members inside the Taunton ground were no less unhappy. The ground here dries well, and there is no doubt the umpires' decision was premature. Hewett, who may have had something to do with that decision, was about to go off to Minehead to play golf for the afternoon with Sammy when the club president decided to placate the members' feelings by asking the umpires to make a new inspection.

At 2 o'clock they decided that the ground was indeed fit for play. The problem was that the Australians were by now relaxing somewhere in the hills. A horseman was hastily sent to try to find them, and the telegraphs were busy between Taunton and the Quantock villages to the same end.

By 4 o'clock the Australians were back ready to play. Somerset, sent in to bat, were dismissed for 119 in under 40 overs. The next day it rained and no play at all was possible, but on the third day a crowd of 5,000 saw some superb bowling by Sammy, on the one side, and Turner on the other, and a result: a win for the visitors by six wickets. Turner took 7 for 26 in Somerset's second-innings total of 64, and in the Australians' two innings on the same day Sammy took 9 of the 14 wickets that fell, for 57 runs.

The crowd was happy at seeing some stirring cricket, but Hewett, the captain, was in a furious mood: not at having lost, rather at what he was said to have regarded as the 'farce' on the first day. He had a big argument with the club officials about the off-on decision. 'The Colonel' was a man of strong views and what had happened rankled with him.

At the end of the season he gave up – a serious loss to Somerset, for he was an outstanding batsman, the country's leading run-scorer the previous season. But as a modern captain, Peter Roebuck, has observed, perhaps Hewett 'had too little self-control to survive as a county captain'. There was quite a bit of criticism in other quarters of the pressures the Somerset officials were said to have exerted on the umpires, who themselves were obviously not blameless in this 'farce'.

That was Hewett's last proper season with Somerset, although he did play for them in one or two more matches in 1894. A new captain was needed, and there was only one man: S.M.J. Woods.

A Man of all Sports

Nearly 40 years after John and Margaret Woods had sailed from Dublin to start their new life in New South Wales, their third son arrived in the Irish capital. He came as a member of the England rugby XV and on a fine afternoon, that of February 7 1891, before a crowd of thousands at the Lansdowne Road ground, he played a prominent role in England's win over Ireland by two tries and three goals to nil. He was to return twice, now as captain, to lead England to further victories.

Sammy's fame as a cricketer, and his long career first as bowler, then as batsman and county captain, tends to overshadow the fact that he was one of the outstanding rugby players of the time. He is remembered today as the forerunner of the modern 'wing forward'. He gained 13 caps for England, in days when there were fewer international games than now (and injury robbed him of more appearances). He also played for two of the most famous clubs in the history of the game: Blackheath and, as a founder member, the Barbarians.

Sammy was also one of the most complete all-round sportsmen of his day, the most versatile, perhaps, to have come out of Australia. Had he also competed in field athletics he might have surpassed Fry in the diversity of his sporting achievements. Had he also not decided to concentrate on rugby, he would have made his name on the soccer field (he played not only for Sussex and Somerset but also had a game or two with the famous Corinthians and for Cambridge). Sammy also captained and played centre-forward for Somerset at hockey; he enjoyed boxing and was at the ringside of most big fights; was a fine golfer and no mean swimmer; played tennis a good deal and took up bowls with enthusiasm, helping to form a club at Bridgwater.

He enjoyed, too, hunting, shooting, and fishing, at all of which he was probably better than he sometimes mockingly pretended. He once told a journalist: 'I am very nearly the worst shot you have ever heard of. At the same time I am by no means dangerous to other guns, and have been known to hit a sitting rabbit. I have shot a keeper and also a dog.' There were also countless games of billiards and skittles when it was time to be indoors.

It was a close friendship with a remarkable sporting family not long after he had settled in Somerset that led to Sammy's getting a job. It was, of all places, in a brewery and it lasted about a couple of years, a lot longer than his previous one in a bank and about as long as his spell, in the 1920s, as the secretary of Somerset county cricket club. Sammy recalled long afterwards: 'I always knew how to drink beer, and still do. But I am afraid I never really learnt the art of making it without the help of Jack Furze, the foreman.'

The family was the Hancocks, of Wiveliscombe, a small town a few miles west of Taunton. Their brewery was one of the biggest in the West of England, and the main local employer. One cannot help but think that Sammy was on the payroll for reasons other than his ability to brew beer. In fact one wonders just how much time he spent working in between his cricket, rugby, and hunting, at all of which the Hancocks seemed as keen as he was. In reality this was perhaps a case of Victorian 'sponsorship'. Sammy rarely had too much money after he left Cambridge, and he was of a generous nature. Although he never amassed material wealth, his essential needs – bed and board, clothes, sporting equipment, and a bottle of this and that – added up to a tidy amount in money. During his time at the brewery he most likely lived at Wiveliscombe, quite possibly with the family.

'What a glorious two years, to be sure!' he said of those days. 'Stag hunting, football, cricket, skittles etc., and we had a lovely pack of foot beagles, so you may imagine we all kept very fit. A wonderful family the Hancocks . . . ten boys and a girl, all fine athletes.' There was a very large garden, in which the boys were always playing rugby and other games.

Once a year they took the beagles to 'Squire Notley's place' at Combe Sydenham. On one visit Sammy was suffering from lumbago, and the Squire recommended his own remedy: to carry a potato or two around with him. (Sammy said it worked, too.) The Squire 'then asked me what I would like to drink. He went to an old tree and produced whisky, brandy, and gin.' Sammy chose gin. Perhaps this was where he got the idea for his caches of drinks on the nearby Quantocks.

Five of the Hancock brothers played rugby for Somerset; one, Phillip Froude, for England; and another, Frank, captained Wales (the family had a brewery in Cardiff, too). At cricket, one brother, William, had a single undistinguished game for Somerset; and Frank's

63

son, Ralph, had several matches for the county before losing his life in France soon after the outbreak of war in 1914. Most of the brothers also played tennis for their county.

Froude was a couple of years older and almost a couple of inches taller than Sammy. On the rugby field his build made him most useful in the line-out. The two were good friends, and it was probably through Froude that Sammy came to play for Blackheath. Froude was also a Cambridge man, but did not get his Blue. To play with the great Blackheath club Froude made the round journey of nearly 350 miles by train in a single day, sometimes having to walk the last 10 miles home from Taunton around midnight. He played for Somerset for many years and on four occasions for England, and toured South Africa in 1891.

Sammy had begun his rugby with the strong Bridgwater club and also turned out for Wellington as well as Wiveliscombe. The latter, dominated by the Hancocks, must have proved exceptionally tough opposition for teams visiting the little town. Sammy got his first county cap while still with Bridgwater, and altogether played for Somerset about 30 times. He captained the county from 1893 to 1896. In his early days he was a threequarter, then a full-back, until moving to the role he is best remembered for, as a wing forward.

He was a master in the art of fast and sure dribbling and relentless tackling. A book published in 1892, *Football, the Rugby Union Game*, recorded that Sammy, as a forward, had a style particularly his own:

> If given a 'roving commission', Woods is one of the most dangerous of forwards. His strength, pace, and dash cause his individual play to be of a most determined character, and though he cannot be termed a scrummager, he has been selected for England on account of the extraordinary pieces of play he is continually bringing off. His tackling is wonderfully sure and exceedingly severe, and in international matches . . . he has frequently been brought out as an extra threequarter to strengthen the defence when England have been pressed on their goal-line.

He was a very hard player. Jessop once joked to him that it was rumoured that 'if an opponent had the choice of two evils, namely, whether to be run over by a motor-car or be tackled by you in a tight match, the latter option would recede to long odds.' Another writer

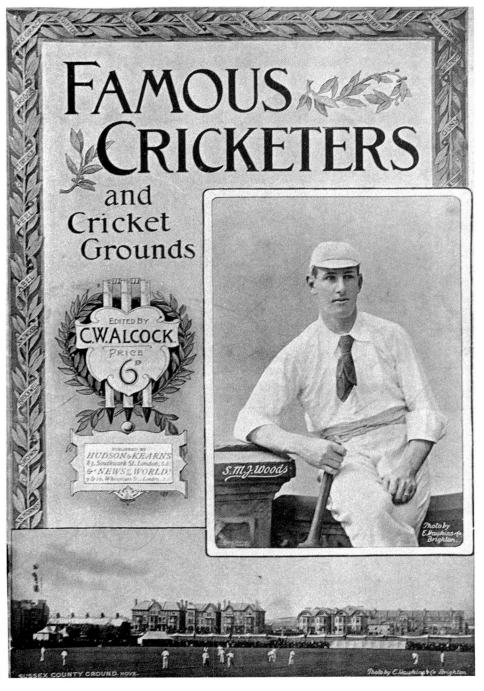

On the cover of the 'Famous Cricketers' series. The ground shown is at Hove, Sussex where Sammy played some big innings.

Bowling for the camera in the days before genuine action pictures.

Gregor MacGregor, Sammy's room-mate at Cambridge and 'perfect partner' on the cricket field. MacGregor later captained Middlesex and played for England.

The *Vanity Fair* cartoon of Sammy by 'Stuff', 1892.

described him going for the line, or for his man, 'with the full fury of a Zulu warrior, whooping to destroy his foe.'

Sammy appeared for Blackheath at various times in the early 1890s, an occasional player rather than a regular. It was in those days by far the strongest club in the country. It boasted so many internationals that on occasions some had to be content with a place in the 2nd XV. When Sammy led out the England team to play Scotland in his last international it included, with himself, nine Blackheath men.

Sammy was a founder member and served on the committee of the most famous rugby club of all, the Barbarians. It dates from a northern tour by a scratch team got together by another Blackheath man, Percy 'Tottie' Carpmael, in 1890. The decision to form the club was taken in a Bradford hotel at 2 o'clock one morning after a long session of eating and drinking by the touring team, which was variously known as 'Carpmael's London team', 'the Southern Nomads', and 'W.P. Carpmael's County and International team'. The Barbarians is a unique club in that it has no ground or clubhouse, and membership is by invitation only (an invitation prized almost as much as one to play for one's country). The club motto is: 'Rugby football is a game for gentlemen in all classes, but never for a bad sportsman in any class'.

The first tour of the new club came that Christmas, and an amusing diary of this, written by one of the team, appeared in a newspaper. It recorded that at 5.30 p.m. on Boxing Day King's Cross Station, London, was 'enlivened' by the presence of members. A list of most of the original Barbarians which followed began with the names of Sammy, his Wiveliscombe chum Froude, and Stoddart, who went on to captain England at both rugby and cricket.

On arrival at Bradford nearly five hours later ('cards on the train') they had supper and changed for a dance which went on into the early hours. Off to Hartlepool for the first match, preceded by 'Melton Mowbray pies and beer. Woods strongly recommends these pies to all players, they should be eaten just before playing . . .' Among those who took part in the match – which the Barbarians won despite the late dance and the pies – was Sammy's Cambridge roommate, MacGregor, who had joined the party in the north. The rugby was interspersed with a good deal of drinking and fun: there is a reference in the diary to 'hair-singeing'. Sammy was in his element.

On the honours board for internationals at Blackheath, in south-east London, the name of S.M.J. Woods appears for 1890, the year he obtained his first England cap. He was then 22, and he might have

65

played the year before but for the dispute between the home rugby countries which kept England out of the international championship for a time.

When internationals were resumed, Sammy made his debut against Wales at Dewsbury on February 15, a game which Wales narrowly won. England's skipper was his friend Stoddart. Sammy played in the other two matches that winter, in which England beat Scotland and Ireland, and quickly established himself as a dominant figure on the field, whether tackling or dribbling down field.

Sammy captained England five times, the first against Ireland at Manchester on February 8, 1892. The crowd of over 12,000 saw a stubbornly-fought game which England won by a goal and a try to nil. Sammy himself converted a try in the second half and immediately headed a rush which led to the second.

This was the year in which England won the triple crown without having a point scored against them. The final match of that series, against Scotland, has been described as more like a cup-tie than an international, with the brandy bottle being frequently used to revive players. It was Sammy who followed up a kick to score the only try, which was converted to give England a 5 – 0 victory and the coveted crown.

In his final season, 1895, Sammy captained England in all three matches. There were victories over Wales at Swansea in January and Ireland back in Dublin in February, but England lost the final encounter (his only defeat as captain) before 20,000 people against Scotland at Richmond. For decades to come Sammy's pack was regarded as the greatest England had had.

Sammy was a great believer in dribbling. When he wrote some advice to players in later years he said: 'It is surprising how easy a rugby ball is to control if only one doesn't try and take it on too quickly.' England lost one match he watched against Wales simply because, he felt, the England pack, supposedly a good one, did not use their feet. Instead, 'they tried to pick up the slimy ball, got bundled over, and on went the Welshmen, still using their feet'. He remembered:

> I had a little parson sitting next to me, and he said, after Wales had got a couple of tries, 'What's the matter, Sam?' I said, 'Our pack can't, or won't, use their feet, and if they don't Wales will get quite a lot of tries yet.' Although he nearly broke the drums of two Welsh enthusiasts' ears in

front of him shouting 'Feet, England, feet! For the Lord's
sake use your feet!' they evidently did not hear the little
fellow's entreaty, for they didn't attempt once during the
game to do so.

Another point on which Sammy held strong views was the need to
break up a scrum immediately the ball had gone and was in the
possession of the other side, and for all to be out and to join the
defence. In his first match as captain, England lost a try through two
of the forwards holding on to him in the scrum and so preventing him
getting out to help in the defence. 'They didn't play for England
again', he added.

Sammy played no more at international level after 1895, and not
much longer for Somerset. There is an amusing account in the *Somerset
County Herald* of how he appeared for the county against Devon in the
game in December 1897 which decided the south-west championship.
Apparently Sammy and Froude Hancock had a week earlier promised
to play, but cried off a couple of days before, pleading that they could
not get fit in time. The newspaper recorded:

> However, an hour or so previous to the time of kick-off
> Woods turned up at the headquarters of the team carrying
> his usual football bag, and though he declared that he had
> no intention of playing, officials and players gathered round
> that bag in the hotel lobby, speculating as to its contents.
> During the luncheon F.H. Fox, who is as wily an official as
> he was a player, persistently plied 'Sammy' with reminis-
> cences of the glorious days of old, when together they used
> to pulverise Devon. His victim began to glow with enthusi-
> asm, and at last, whilst unlacing one boot, significantly asked
> whether it was possible to borrow a pair of pants anywhere.
> This was enough! Willing hands quickly pulled off the other
> boot, and although it was within half-an-hour of kick-off
> 'Sammy' was rigged up in becoming attire, the mysterious
> bag supplying all deficiencies, and for the sixteenth time he
> appeared in the field against his county's oldest rivals . . .

Alas, he could not stave off the defeat which had been forecast,
Devon winning by 6 points to nil. The other local paper, the *Gazette*,
bluntly declared that his appearance was not in the best interests of
Somerset as he was just 'not fit', and said:

Twice he made characteristic tackles, and once or twice dribbled well, but he was not the Sammy of old, and having been relegated to the shelf it would be far better to stay there than finish a brilliant football career by appearing as an 'old crock'.

The 'old crock' was 30, and the rugby reporter was right. It was another nine or ten years before he gave up altogether, though, and until then played both rugby and soccer 'on and off' at a less serious level.

Sammy was an avid follower of boxing. He would be at the ringside at big matches, and while at Cambridge he paid a boxer named Galpin to spar with him. Once the famous one-time prizefighter Jem Mace, the 'Swaffham Gipsy', and his cousin Pooley Mace were giving exhibition shows at a circus. Sammy and several others paid Jem £5 to box with them. But Jem 'was getting on in years and was a little too fond of "gargle"', Sammy recalled. Pooley, however, Sammy saw quite a bit of and rated him a fine instructor. Galpin was a little annoyed at this, but was perhaps mollified when he got paid as usual.

A newspaper article, headed 'S.M.J. Woods, the Superman', recalled a confrontation he had with an unnamed 'famous heavy-weight professional champion'. This boxer, for some reason, barred the way on a steamer taking Sammy and the England XV on one of their visits to Dublin. Sammy thereupon knocked the man down. (Afterwards they had a drink or two together.) As someone once said, Sammy was a good one to have with you in a scrap.

Sammy also played mixed hockey for a time, and was not entirely joking when he said he thought it more dangerous than rugby. His injuries included a broken thumb and 'a very bad hit on the knee from a lady' which kept him out of county cricket for a month. In a couple of years as Somerset's captain and centre-forward he did not lose a match.

Sammy wrote later that 'although I am a firm believer in girls having lots of exercise, I don't think hockey is a woman's game.' A little remininiscent of what Grace said after two teams of 'Lady cricketers' had given exhibition matches round the country in 1891: 'Cricket is not a game for women, and although the fair sex occa-sionally join in a picnic game, they are not constitutionally adapted for the sport.'

At about the time Somerset became a first-class cricket county one of the best-known golf courses was being opened on rabbit-infested sand dunes at Burnham-on-Sea, a few miles from Bridgwater. Sammy decided to take up the game, and was fortunate in having as his instructor the great J.H. Taylor, soon to be British open champion. Burnham was then a small nine-hole course.

Taylor, 'a most charming fellow', in his early twenties, was the club's first professional. He and Sammy got to know each other quite well. Part of Taylor's duties was the sale of 'liquor' between 1 and 2 and 4 and 5. Taylor taught Sammy 'not to hit the ball as you do at cricket', and Sammy got down to a handicap of two. But after a year or two Sammy ceased to take the game seriously, although he played a good deal for many years. Burnham was one of his favourite haunts in his middle age, and here, too, legend has it, he would produce a bottle or two previously hidden at strategic points round the course.

'Shamateur' Captain

S ammy took over the captaincy of Somerset at the start of the 1894 season after Hewett's decision to give up. He led the county for 13 summers, making him their longest-serving captain. In the same period he was on more overseas tours – to South Africa, the West Indies, and again to North America – and he was playing for (and eventually captaining) the Gentlemen in their annual encounters with the Players. And when there was no first-class match, he was more than happy to turn out for Bridgwater or play in a country-house or even a village match.

As captain of Somerset, his most difficult task often was in assembling a decent team; indeed there were times when he was hard put to get together a team at all. There was a handful of dependable players, but otherwise the side consisted of ever-changing amateurs of questionable ability.

For most of his years as captain Sammy was also the club's joint secretary. This was an appointment which was nothing more than a way of paying him for his cricket and keeping him in Somerset (and probably, in fact, in this country at all). He became one of England's cricket 'shamateurs'.

W.G. Grace is the best-known 'shamateur'. One biographer has estimated that he grossed £120,000 from cricket, which needs to be multiplied many times to give the equivalent figure in today's terms. Many other 'amateurs' were paid comparatively well in one way or another: for jobs they did not do, expenses, testimonials, even expensive wedding gifts.

Joe Darling, the Australian captain at the turn of the century, considered that 'very few' of the English amateurs in his time were truly amateur, but were 'highly paid professionals'. He would have been referring only to the top cricketers who played more or less all the time, such as the ones he cited (notably Grace, Stoddart, MacLaren, and Jessop) and not to the larger number of lesser players who appeared irregularly. It is an aspect of the game usually ignored in cricket histories, but in a chapter, 'The Disguised Professional', in

70

his book, *The Players*, Ric Sissons says it was clear that the M.C.C. and county committees either turned a blind eye or were directly involved.

When he became captain, Sammy was elected joint hon. secretary, along with Henry Murray-Anderdon. A village squire with an aristocratic style, Murray-Anderdon had been hon. secretary for some time and continued to do an immense amount of work for the young club for many years to come. Why Sammy was given this honorary office at this point and what he did is not clear: perhaps there was a slight extension of his duties as captain. But in 1898, while Murray-Anderdon continued as hon. secretary, doubtless doing all the real secretarial work, Sammy was appointed as simply joint secretary, the honorary part of the title disappearing.

The minutes of the annual meeting that year record that Mr. H.H. Palairet said that 'the committee considered it advisable to have a paid secretary, with a salary of £200 per annum.' After 'some discussion' this was agreed. At a later time, perhaps at the next annual meeting, the words 'in interests of club' were added in the minutes after the word 'advisable'. It was obviously a delicate matter, and the words had to be right.

However, the reporter from the *Somerset County Gazette* was there with his shorthand and took down the words of Mr Palairet in proposing the appointment. They show the reason: 'It was really (he said) a question of whether they would lose his services or not, and he did not think Somerset could afford to do without him.' So it was not that a paid secretary was needed but that Sammy would otherwise probably have had to go back to Australia. It is known that he had to consider returning there (albeit not willingly) two or three times.

The man with the job of getting the move accepted by the meeting, Henry Hamilton Palairet, an old Etonian keen on hunting, shooting, and fishing, had played for the M.C.C. in one or two first-class fixtures and was for some years champion archer of England. He is best remembered, though, as father of the cricketing brothers Lionel and Richard.

Sammy kept the £200-a-year sinecure for the rest of the time he was captain; and he was also given a handsome testimonial, something that came the way of few amateurs.

The decision to pay him did not go unnoticed nationally. In *Sporting Life*, 'Old Blue' wrote in his column:

> I dare swear that a few years ago 'good old Sammy' would have laughed at the idea of his present position. With so

many examples of 'making cricket pay' before his eyes, however, he has (wisely perhaps) accepted the inevitable and – in this case – 'the labourer is truly worth his hire' . . . Not only is he *facile princeps* in every department of the grand old game, but he is a heaven-born captain. His very presence in any team has the same rousing effect of Taillefer in the Battle of Hastings. All the same, like Dr. Grace, Mr. Woods' position is anomalous on the face of it; that is, of course, if he still claims the title of gentleman-amateur.

Back to the cricket field (Sammy was no office wallah): within a year or two of taking over as captain, his bowling, alas, was ceasing to be the terror to batsmen that it had been in the late 1880s and early 1890s. 'I have to pretend I'm bowling now,' he was to joke; and at the time he received his testimonial cheque in 1907 he said, 'I am sorry my bowling went off the way it did so quickly.' But as his bowling declined, his batting noticeably improved. In his younger days in first-class cricket he had tended to 'have a go' before taking the measure of the bowling. Although he was an aggressive batsman who revelled in hitting his way out of trouble, he was also, if necessary, excellent in defence.

Sammy had a good eye, and was a fine, forcing, fast-footed driver with a powerful square cut. He was also adept at the Victorian draw stroke, deflecting a ball on or near the leg stump, his bat held slant-wise, so that it passed between wicket and legs and usually meant four runs to fine long leg. He was one of the most successful and last exponents of this rather risky stroke, and used it against some of the fastest bowlers.

In his *The Charm of Cricket Past and Present*, C.H.B. Pridham wrote of Sammy's 'fantastic footwork', and observed that he was apt to use the draw stroke when things were looking black for his side. His main object may have been 'to annoy the bowlers'.

One of the countless cartoons of Sammy around the turn of the century shows him executing a variation of the draw stroke. It bears the legend: 'The Surrey cut. A favourite stroke.' An audacious one, too, for the cartoon shows that Sammy, standing to the leg side of the wicket, has just deflected the ball *between* his legs.

In an interview a year or two before becoming captain, Sammy confessed that although usually not in the slightest nervous and never when bowling, he sometimes felt a little apprehensive when going in to bat. Surprisingly these were on occasions when there was no need to be – when there was no crisis, or when playing in a local club match (when, of course, he was expected to hit the bowling about).

He also confessed in the same interview to being superstitious about batting at No. 6 – something he said he disliked intensely. He blamed it on a bad run of luck in his school days when he went in at that spot. He must have grown out of this, for later on he frequently batted at No. 6 when he was captain, and produced some good innings. In his long career he batted at some time or another at every place in the order. Sometimes he liked to open, but generally was most successful halfway down.

Sammy's arrival at the wicket always created attention. There were fewer, if any, in his day who were quicker at reaching the crease. He bustled out from the pavilion, swinging his bat, and more than once he ran. He was also very keen on the 'short run' – in the sense of taking a quick run when the ball was hit only a short distance. 'There is hardly anything in the world I enjoy so much as doing a short run successfully,' he once said. He often unbalanced the fielders with this 'tip and run' tactic, so much that their wild throws resulted in many extra runs. It also, of course, resulted in plenty of run outs. Indeed he admitted that he probably ran out more partners than most other batsmen.

'Plum' Warner, looking back on Sammy as a batsman, wrote that although he was no stylist, he was a very powerful driver and leg hitter and also cut square well. The greatness of his batting, however, lay in his 'greatness of heart'. And C.B. Fry, writing while Sammy was at the peak of his batting career, called him 'the Ajax of the cricket field'. He kept his bat very straight, Fry said, and most of his strokes were powerful drives.

At the same time, the Hon. R.H. Lyttleton wrote:

> Woods cannot be described as a correct bat, and if he has to play good bowling on a difficult wicket he does not attempt to play a safe game, but goes for the bowling with the utmost courage, and his magnificent eye often enables him to triumph over both ground and the bowlers.

Sammy was also a superb fielder at almost any position, especially at cover-point or extra mid-off. Warner rated him as 'a very great mid-off', making some wonderful catches there off the slow bowling of Somerset's Tyler. He had big, safe hands, and if he could not get the ball with his hands would stop a hot drive with his shins rather than let there be a run. A precept as captain was 'The nearer the game, the greater the knowledge', and this sometimes led him to stand at silly point. When someone pointed out that it was a suicidal position and that he might get killed (he wore no protection), he replied: 'Well, you only die once, and I would as soon pass out that way as any other.' Archie MacLaren thought him the finest silly point of all.

Sammy's first season as captain, 1894, was successful enough: indeed one of the best he had. In the county championship, Somerset won six, lost seven, and drew three matches, and climbed a couple of places in the table. But, ominously, no fewer than 28 players turned out for the county, and the team was constantly changing. 'Sometimes I was hard pressed to get an eleven,' he said. 'Still we were a happy party and knew how to take a licking.' Apart from himself and two or three others among the amateurs (including Henry Palairet's talented boys) and the two reliable professionals, Tyler and Nichols, there was little depth to the side.

Two defeats were humiliating: at Manchester on July 17 Somerset were dismissed for 31 and defeated by an innings in the same day; and only two days later, at Huddersfield, Yorkshire also inflicted an innings defeat in a single day. Earlier in the season the visiting South Africans, albeit not a formidable side, had been beaten by nine wickets at Taunton; and other successes included victory over Kent at Canterbury in a match when Sammy took 12 wickets. That summer he took 53 wickets for the county at 18.4. By coincidence his batting average was also 18.4.

Although the following year was no more successful for the county, it was a season which still stands out for performances both for and against Somerset. In this summer of 1895 MacLaren hit his record-breaking 424 off the toiling bowlers at Taunton; Grace made his 100th first-class century off the same attack; and Sammy, in the course of reaching 1,000 runs in a season for the first time, hit the fastest double-century recorded up to then in the first-class game. And Somerset demonstrated their ability to be 'the team of surprises' by another in a series of defeats of the team of the decade, the county champions Surrey.

First came Grace's century of centuries. It was in May when Somerset travelled to Bristol to meet Gloucester. Sammy recalled:

> We scored 200 for 1 wicket. W.G. then went on and took 5
> wickets, and we were all out for 300. He then proceeded to
> go in first and helped himself to 288, and to get his 100th

hundred. I had the satisfaction of giving him a full pitch to get to his hundred, not that he wanted any help, and it was the proudest moment of my cricket career to have been the one to do so.

Both Grace and Sammy were uncharacteristically suffering a bit from nerves as the great man neared his 100. Charles Townsend, who was at the wicket with Grace much of the time, said: 'This was the one and only time I ever saw him flustered, when the last runs were needed.' He added: 'Poor Sam Woods could hardly bowl the ball and the Doctor was nearly as bad.'

According to Robertson-Glasgow, Sammy believed he had Grace plumb lbw when he was on three or four, but after that he did not give a chance until he was caught off Sammy just short of his triple century. That early miss was the only time Sammy beat Grace's bat. The clerical wicketkeeper, Archie Wickham, related that he had only four balls to take all the time Grace was facing the bowlers. Gloucester won easily (but Sammy got his revenge in the corresponding match the next year, hitting a century and half-century to give Somerset victory).

Grace, who was then nearly 47, hit 38 fours, of which quite a few would have counted as six had the rule not then been that the ball had to be struck right out of the ground.

There was a celebration dinner for Grace after the match. Sammy remembered:

> He drank something of everything before and during dinner, and afterwards he sent for the whisky. You couldn't make the Old Man drunk. His nut was too large. About midnight, some of us thought we might start for home; but the Old Man said to me: 'Shock'head, get two others, and we'll play rubbers of whist till 2.' So we did.

It was Sammy's turn next to enter the record books with the fastest double-century. He had already scored 180 against Cambridge early in that season, and then in June he hit 109, 215, and 85 in successive innings. The century (before lunch) was on the third day of the match against Middlesex at Lord's; the double-century off Sussex at Brighton; the 85 off Surrey. Through his career he was fond of the Sussex bowlers. Six of his 19 first-class centuries came off them, three at Brighton, where he had been to school.

On this occasion it was a captain-to-the-rescue innings. Sussex had made over 500, and Somerset lost four wickets and had not reached 100 when Sammy went into action.

He made 50 in just under half an hour, a mixture of hitting and 'tip and run'; 100 in 80 minutes; 200 in 135 minutes. He was out to a catch in the deep, having scored 215 out of 282 added in the two and a half hours he was at the wicket. He hit 32 fours, mostly drives. One ball was deposited into the pavilion. 'I hit fours to save my legs,' he joked.. He gave two chances, neither easy, in his 40s: one a difficult one to slip, the other a skied ball over point which three fielders tried to reach. The match ended in a draw, its total runs also creating a record: 1,344 was the highest aggregate in a county match.

Sammy's innings stood as the fastest double-century for eight years until Jessop reached 200 in just 120 minutes – again, as it happens, on a visit to Sussex. Sammy was a great admirer of Jessop's and had seen his potential in his very first season with Gloucester in 1894. Grace at the time asked Sammy his opinion of the 20-year-old, and Sammy replied that he had 'the eye of an eagle' and was going to make 'lots of runs'.

Back to that season of records. Sammy and his fellow bowlers and fielders had a very busy time at the beginning of July. In successive games at Taunton they lost to Essex by an innings and 317 runs, and to Lancashire by an innings and 452. 'A nice week's cricket, don't you think' he remarked. It was in the latter match that MacLaren amassed 424 of Lancashire's total of 801; beating Grace's record of 344, which had stood for almost 20 years, as the highest innings in first-class cricket. MacLaren's record was not broken for games in England until Brian Lara's epic innings of 501 not out for Warwickshire against Durham 99 years later.

MacLaren, who batted for just under eight hours, hit one ball out of the ground for six and 62 fours. Sammy called it a 'marvellous' innings and noted only one chance, when MacLaren was on 228. Wickham failed to hold a catch behind the stumps.

In that week's 'nice cricket' Sammy had given a trial to a 17-year-old Wellington lad, Herbert Gamlin, an off-break bowler who, he had observed, had been taking a lot of cheap wickets at club level. It was hardly the right baptism for him, and he had only one more game for Somerset, concentrating instead on rugby and, like Sammy, playing for both Blackheath and England. Gamlin became one of the greatest full-backs, nicknamed 'The Octopus'. In his brief county cricket career he took two wickets for 207 runs, both in that Lancashire match. And one was that of MacLaren, albeit a catch in the deep off a not very good delivery. 'Still, he was no worse than the rest of the bowlers,' said Sammy in looking back on that match, in which his own figures were 2 for 163.

For the first time a Somerset bowler took 100 wickets in a season in championship matches. But it was Tyler, not Sammy, whose own tally of 61 cost just over 27 runs apiece. He blamed things on a strained leg which caused him trouble through the season. With the bat, though, he scored 1,405 in all his first-class innings, an average of over 34. That winter he was chosen for Lord Hawke's England party for South Africa, and played in the three Tests there.

The 'team of surprises' provided several shocks through the 1890s for high-riding Surrey, team of the decade and champions more often than not. In his book *Background to Cricket*, Sir Home Gordon wrote that some of his friend Sammy's innings at the Oval were 'inspired by his avowed hatred of his opponents and their supporters'. Sir Home was exaggerating. Sammy did not think much of the Surrey establishment ('The committee at the Oval don't know a player from a doll' he said of Surrey's decision to let go some talented players). But that is not the same as hating the Surrey players and spectators. Indeed in his reminiscences Sammy said the Oval crowd 'always gave us a splendid reception and behaved as thorough sportsmen, whether we won or lost.'

A cause of animosity between the two counties arose over the future great all-rounder, Len Braund. Surrey had surprisingly let him go after he had played occasionally for them, and Somerset welcomed him. There was some trouble over his qualification, however, and complaints were made to Lord's. Sammy, who was no lover of red tape and officialdom in general, brought things to a head by including Braund in his team to play Middlesex at Lord's in 1900. It was ruled firmly that Braund must not play for Somerset for another season.

But if some feeling did exist between Sammy and the Surrey powers-that-be as a result, which might have given him extra incentive to do well in their encounters, it does not have any bearing on Somerset's triumphs in the 1890s, for these preceded the Braund affair.

At the Oval in late August 1895, lowly Somerset outplayed the champions to win by 53 runs in a match memorable for Tyler's taking all 10 wickets in the first innings (for which he was rewarded by a collection totalling over £35). The following August Sammy and his men did it again, defeating Surrey in the latter's last match of the season. Then in 1897 they beat Surrey twice and by the second victory at Taunton late in the summer deprived them of the championship. In the earlier match that season, at the Oval, Somerset had been victorious by 224 runs, with Sammy hitting 88 and being the top scorer on either side.

At the Oval in May 1899 Surrey, batting first, scored 811 (Bobby Abel contributed 357) and defeated Somerset by an innings and 379. But the next year Sammy got his revenge – and it was now that the Braund affair may have provided that extra edge – by beating Surrey twice. Sammy scored another century in the second of these matches.

But these were rare triumphs, sweet as they were. In spite of Sammy's efforts, Somerset were finishing near the bottom – sometimes at the bottom – of the table. The championship had been enlarged in 1895 by the admission of five more counties (Derby, Essex, Hampshire, Leicester, and Warwicks) and was further increased during his captaincy, in 1899 by Worcester and in 1905 Northants.

Somerset had won six matches in each of 1894 and 1895, but in the next four years managed only nine altogether. In 1898 they had just one win, and it was defeat after defeat. The fault was hardly Sammy's – the county lacked bowling strength, and the batting was often uncertain. The trouble was that there were few good enough players regularly in the team.

In his years as captain Sammy often used as many as 30 players in a season, and rarely did the same team play twice. Things got even worse in the new century, and in Sammy's last year for the county (1910) he was one of no fewer than 38 who represented Somerset. The problem, especially for the less well-off counties, was that professionals cost more money than amateurs who, apart from a few 'shamateurs' like Sammy, received at most their expenses.

Jessop, who succeeded Grace as captain of Gloucester, had the same problem in finding enough players and knew well enough how a few of what Sammy termed 'rabbits' from time to time crept into a team. One cricketer Sammy played against Gloucester was so out of his depth that Jessop asked why he was being used. 'Oh,' said Sammy, 'he can't bat; he doesn't bowl, and he ain't much of a field, but he's helluva golfer.' Lord Hawke had a similar tale about when Sammy took 'a funny sort of Somerset side' to Yorkshire. 'Well, Sam, who are all these fellows? I don't seem to know them. Are they useful cricketers?' Sammy replied without hesitation: 'As cricketers they are not much use, but they are damned good shots.'

It was a big headache for Sammy (and Jessop and others), but he could joke about it. Robertson-Glasgow related how Sammy used to tell how he was captaining a Somerset side in the North, and found himself three short. So, Sammy said, stretching the truth slightly, as he often did,

> I picked up a couple of my godsons, who had nothing better to do; and that made ten. With which we started by train. On the way I got talking to a fellow who said he'd made hundreds and hundreds in club cricket. So I made him our 11th man. He made nought and nought, and it turned out he hadn't played since he was ten, but wanted to get a close view of the game for nothing.

The term 'rabbits' was popular around the turn of the century for describing batsmen of little ability, of whom Somerset had more than its fair share. Sammy was very fond of the word; and indeed is credited by F. Hanson Haig in his book *Ashes and Rubber* with having invented its cricketing use. Somerset always had a long tail, and after the third wicket had fallen Sammy would say, 'We now open the hatch and out come the rabbits.' Sammy even extended the term to bowler and fielders who were not up to it, and once applied the word to himself. Writing of a time when he was taking few wickets and getting out for low scores, he called himself a 'Brer rabbit'.

Sammy may no longer have been a bowler to fear, and Somerset may have lacked the strength to do much of note other than to surprise Surrey, but his performances with the bat were a bright part of the story of the closing years of the century. From 1895 to 1900 he hit 11 centuries for the county, and would have reached 1,000 runs more than three times in this period but for injuries. Surprisingly his first home century did not come until August 1898, when he took 144 off the Kent bowlers at Taunton and set a seventh-wicket record for Somerset, which stood for nearly a century. His partner was Vernon Hill, a cheery Oxford blue and a left-hander noted for his hard hitting. Together they put on 240. By coincidence, when the record was broken at Bath in June 1996 one of those responsible was a young Australian all-rounder, Shane Lee, of New South Wales.

These were days when a good deal of long-forgotten verse about cricket and cricketers found itself in print in the sporting periodicals and newspapers. This alphabetical eulogy by an anonymous 'poet' is one of several featuring Sammy at about this time:

A for the *Activity* shown when at play,
Batting and *Bowling* are never astray,
C for the *Centuries* often scored,
D for the *Duck's egg* he never once scored,
E for his *Efficiency* ruling the team,
F for his *Fielding*, that's just like a dream,
G for the *Grand* way he handles his bat,
H for his *Head* of hair, thick as a mat,
I for his *Innings*, none are better than his,
J for the *Jolly* good fellow he is,
K for the *Knowledge* he has of the game,
L for the *Ladies* that acknowledge his fame,
M for the *Maidens* he bowls by the score,
Never was seen such a player before!
O, his *Opponents*, he scatters them all,
P for his *Pads*, seldom touched by the ball,
Q for the *Quality* rare of his bowling,
R for the *Run* ere he sets the ball rolling,
S is for *Sammy*, all Somerset's pride,
T for the *Treasure* he is to his side,
U for his *Unequalled* length of limb,
V for the *Vigour* displayed by him,
W for the *Wonderful* way that he catches,
X for his *Xcellence*, shown in our matches,
Y for his *Youth*, on whom so much depends,
Z for the *Zeal* which on cricket he spends.

A few weeks before the record stand with Hill, Sammy produced a match-winning performance with both bat and ball to provide what *Wisden* called 'a sensational finish' at Eastbourne. Rain prevented play on the first day, and after Somerset had been dismissed for 133 and Sussex had replied with 202 a victory for the visitors seemed unlikely. But opening the batting, Sammy hit 143 (out of 173 while he was at the wicket) and Sussex were left with a target of 219. With less than two hours to go, a draw seemed inevitable. But some fine bowling by Tyler had Sussex in trouble, then Sammy took three of the last five wickets for 10 runs to give his team victory by 108 runs. It was their only success of the season.

Sammy took another century (109) off Sussex the following year, 1899, in a drawn match at Taunton in which 1,293 runs were scored for only 26 wickets. A remarkable feature was that all the Somerset players, including the wicketkeeper, bowled, and all but three of the Sussex team, too. Sammy hit three centuries that summer, the others being 111 against Kent at Tonbridge, and 146 against Lancashire at Taunton.

In contrast to the high-scoring match against Sussex was that against Middlesex at Lord's the same season, in which Somerset scored 35 and 44 and lost by an innings and seven runs. Rain prevented play on the first day, and it was all over in just over three hours of playing time on the second. At one point in their second innings Somerset were 8 for 8 after four overs and were saved from recording the lowest first-class score only by a defiant 20 from Sammy.

In the county matches of 1899 he scored 1,110 runs at an average of 42.69, but he took a mere 21 wickets and they cost more than 35 runs each.

It was often remarked how Sammy played a captain's innings when his side were in trouble. A frequent spectator at matches in which he played, Perceval Graves, wrote this account of one such occasion, also against Middlesex at Lord's:

> The wicket was a 'sticky dog' and too many batsmen were getting themselves out through groping for the ball instead of going for it. Sam Woods, padded up and prepared to face the music, was enjoying a double whisky and a Burmese cheroot, scarcely a combination suitable for the average cricketer. Thoroughly in his element, J.T. Hearne was carrying all before him, breaking both ways and making the ball come quickly off the pitch. Another wicket had fallen. 'This must stop' growled the captain as he stooped down to change his white buckskin boots for that piebald pair he loved so well. In he strode, took guard (I think it was 'leg stump') and gave a swift but comprehensive glance all round the wicket. Quite unaware of what was coming to him, Hearne continued to keep an impeccable length. But his next three deliveries, that pitched not far outside the off stump, were flailed with lusty vigour to the leg boundary . . . The skipper went on from strength to strength, punishing every loose ball as well as maintaining a strong defence, and compiled over 70 before he was caught napping.

His matches for Somerset – and the rest of his first-class appearances, for the Gentlemen and other representative teams – were by no means Sammy's only cricket. He played in local club games, mostly for what was now his 'home' town of Bridgwater. His huge hitting, including a double century in 95 minutes against Burnham in 1898, delighted the spectators. They were amused, too, by the wily lobs with which he sometimes claimed wickets.

He enjoyed his local cricket and the company of his local friends, and was so keen that he was known to travel down from Yorkshire on a Friday night to play a game with Bridgwater on the Saturday; then back by train on Sunday to resume Somerset's northern tour on the Monday. Once, a finger having been damaged in a county match, he had it put in a splint and turned out for Bridgwater. The club made him their captain from 1898 and although he could usually manage only a few games a year played for them until 1919.

Sometimes he would bring one or two county players with him to appear for Bridgwater, both to boost the side and give the crowd a treat. (On one occasion it was announced that he was bringing W.G. Grace, but neither he nor the doctor arrived.) His motives were understandable, but unfortunately it meant that local men had to be dropped from the team, sometimes at the last moment. The time had to come, though this was much later, when the secretary had the unenviable task, on behalf of the committee, of asking Sammy not to do so; and this hastened the day when his close association with the Bridgwater club came to an end.

The late Albert Lock, who served Bridgwater C.C. for very many years as player, secretary, and groundsman, was one of those who turned up to play and had to stand down because Sammy had brought along one or two county players. Another of Albert's memories was how Sammy and some friends used on a Friday night to take a barrel of beer from the club into the nearby Quantock Hills. Then, on the Saturday, they would have a night there playing cards and drinking.

Sammy's cricket often also took him to Quantock Lodge, near Nether Stowey, in the hills near Bridgwater. 'Lodge' may give the impression of a small country property, but Quantock Lodge was built on the grand scale (it later became a hospital and is now a boarding school). It was erected in 1857 in the Elizabethan style for the first and only Lord Taunton, the Whig M.P. Henry Labouchere. It subsequently became the home of the Stanley family, Edward Stanley, Tory M.P. for Bridgwater for many years, having married Lord Taunton's daughter.

Stanley was keen on cricket, and his sons arranged many matches there on the lovely ground in which well-known county players, mostly from Somerset and Gloucester, took part. His elder son, Henry, a useful middle-order batsman, played 50 games for Somerset under Sammy's captaincy.

Sammy was often a guest at the house. He was more in tune with the two sons than with the M.P., who was something of a classical scholar. One night when Sammy was staying there he went down to the library to get his pipe and found Edward Stanley reading one of his favourite authors. Sammy returned upstairs, concerned that at this late hour 'the old gent is working'. To Sammy a book in Latin could bring back only unhappy memories of 'work'.

In Bridgwater Sammy was a popular hero and while he could mix with the Stanley family and their friends he was just as happy at home with the ordinary folk. One elderly resident recalled to the author that his father had revered Sammy as 'a god'. It mattered not to Sammy that Bridgwater, a mainly working-class town, was rather looked down on by the county town of Taunton. Perhaps its spirit of independence appealed to him. One wonders what he felt when in 1896 during a three-month strike by brickmakers there was rioting in Bridgwater and troops were called in from the Plymouth garrison.

Apart from enthusiastically riding in a pair-horse carriage with postilion in the grand carnival parade for some years, Sammy took a leading role in other spheres of the town's social life. Whenever the Bridgwater cricket club's funds were low, as was often the case, a smoking concert would be arranged and he would do his musical turn. He made quite a name for himself as a humorous vocalist, and always got a tumultuous welcome when he appeared on the platform. Albert Chevalier's cockney songs and ballads were his forté. For years he was the star turn at the annual carnival entertainment, and also often organised concerts for deserving causes in the district. C.B. Fry believed that 'had Sammy Woods devoted himself to the music-hall stage, he would have made a fortune.'

These must have been some of his happiest days, rivalling those at Cambridge. In the winter, too, there were rugby and soccer; and in the closing years of the century there were three more overseas cricket tours as well.

South Africa and West Indies

In the winter of 1895–96 Sammy was a member of a strong party of 14 which Lord Hawke took to South Africa. It was a successful tour on the cricket field, England easily winning the three Tests; but off the field it was disrupted by a volatile political situation, a tremendous explosion in Johannesburg, and accidents and illness among the players. Sammy started off with a strained shoulder which curtailed his bowling, but despite a strained leg he contributed some useful innings. As might be expected, he seems to have been the life and soul of the party. He also had a somewhat strange encounter with the Boer leader, Kruger.

Cricket was then in its infancy in South Africa. The England party was the strongest to visit the colony, almost all its members having played regularly at first-class level. For most, however, it was their first taste of Test cricket. Those making their debut included Hawke himself; C.B. Fry, the great Sussex all-round sportsman; and Tom Hayward, the Surrey professional, for many years to be one of England's top batsmen and at that time a useful bowler, too.

For Sammy, already a Test player for Australia, it provided his debut for England, making him the fourth of the five Australians who have appeared for both countries. There were a couple of his Somerset colleagues also in the party: Hewett and the professional, Tyler. The latter, in spite of promising performances with his slow left-arm deliveries (Fry rated him as good as Hedley Verity), played in only one Test in his career, the last of this tour.

There were a couple of other professionals: George Lohmann, the Surrey medium-fast bowler, who was the bowling hero in South Africa, taking three times as many wickets as anyone else; and Sussex's Harry Butt, wicketkeeper. The other amateurs were Arthur Hill and Christopher Heseltine (Hampshire), Sir Tim O'Brien and Hugh Bromley-Davenport (Middlesex), 'Chawles' Wright (Nottingham), and Audley Miller, an old Etonian who captained Wiltshire.

The tour did not start well, with a foretaste of some of the disruptions and mishaps to come. Hawke, Hewett, and O'Brien travelled separately, and their vessel, the Union Castle mail ship *Moor* was delayed, making them miss the first match. The main party had arrived in Cape Town on December 22 in the Intermediate liner *Goth*. Fry recalled: 'My education was much advanced by sharing a cabin with Sammy Woods.' Sammy had only one rival in the cricketing world for telling stories, Fry reckoned, this being 'Chawles' Wright, who had also been with Sammy on his earlier tour to North America.

Sammy recorded 'a funny experience' at Tenerife, on the way out:

> We had dinner ashore. Harry Butt, Ted Tyler, and Tom Hayward were in a crowded boat ready to go to the ship. Some of our party hadn't paid their fare and the boatmen were Portugese, I fancy, about five feet tall. We were up in the bows, lying under a wharf six feet high. I sang out 'Push her off', when one of the beauties hit me on the head with a boat-hook. I had a basket full of guaves I had brought with me. I could throw in those days, and hit him twice in the face. Such a mess his face was in. Then some of his friends began throwing timber at us, when I put my hand in my pocket and caught hold of my pipe and pretended it was a revolver and threatened to shoot. Those in the boat pushed off and we got aboard. Tom Hayward, Tyler, and Butt were in a devil of a fright.

The party spent Christmas Day climbing part of the way up Table Mountain, and then on Boxing Day came the first match. It was played over two days on the lovely Newlands ground, against 15 of Western Province, and the tourists were beaten. They also narrowly lost a one-day match the next day, this time Western Province playing only 11 men. However, there was to be no question about the third match, against 13 of Cape Colony. Hawke's men scored over 400 (with 148 from Fry and 89 from Sammy) and comfortably won by an innings; and they were not to lose any more of their 18 fixtures.

The matches were mostly played on matting wickets, and the tourists also had to get used quickly to the light, which they found trying to the eyes. At first it made the judging of high catches very difficult. Sammy was to start with nonplussed by the deceptive atmosphere. 'Mine,' he drawled confidently from mid-off as he saw the ball coming down his throat. But it fell a foot in front of him.

The tourists were to have had lunch with Cecil Rhodes. They certainly had a very good lunch, but not with him, for news of the Jameson Raid had come to Rhodes in his office in Cape Town. Jameson had led a party of police into Transvaal in support of the dissatisfied 'Vitlanders', the non-Boer whites, hoping it would coincide with an uprising; but the incursion was a failure. This meant the first change in the programme for Hawke's men. There was a break of a few days, with a good deal of uncertainty owing to the political crisis, and the party were left kicking their heels. Then they were tele-graphed to go to Johannesburg, a 1,000-mile train journey away. In that unhappy city, it was hoped the cricket would provide some relief, and turn people's minds from the raid.

On the way, at the Transvaal frontier station, a line of burghers with loaded rifles met the party, who had to pay duty even on their cricket bats. 'The Colonel', Hewett, nearly caused a serious incident, for an official thought he had a revolver in a trousers pocket.

Hewett, an obdurate man, declined to be searched, and adopted a threatening attitude. There were a few noisy moments, though Hewett himself remained silently negative. Armed men joined the scene, and things looked ugly. However, Hawke, with his talent for tact, defused the situation. Hewett was allowed to get off the train with the others – with a cylindrical toothbrush bottle still in his trousers pocket, unexamined. Shortly after this Hewett returned early to England for business reasons. Sammy's other Somerset team-mate, Tyler, also missed several matches (and a likely earlier Test debut) through sickness.

A few miles outside Johannesburg the toursts heard a tremendous explosion. Three trucks of dynamite in a station siding had blown up, causing much damage and many casualties. At their hotel they found the water supply had been cut off by commandos, and had to wash in soda-water. Boer artillery was on points of advantage overlooking the town. The cricket ground where they were to play was used as a temporary hospital. The three-day match in Johannesburg ended in a draw, but Hawke wrote: 'We certainly fulfilled the reason of our visit, for over £800 was taken at the gate.'

After a few days they were sent to Pretoria, of all places, where the Boer leader Paul Kruger, president of the Transvaal, was sitting in 'saturnine triumph', as Fry put it. Sammy, Fry, and one or two others rode out to where Jameson's men had been cornered. Sammy was given a known buck-jumper to ride, it being forgotten that he was an Australian. Sammy was hurt, but not from falling off. He said: 'I suppose you think that this blighter can buck. Let me tell you he's only a pig-rooter.'

Hawke's men, it was now decided, should call on Kruger, and early one morning, in small groups, they were ushered into a room in his villa. Sammy did not consider his own interview worth recording in his reminiscences, but Fry, so anxious to get a good look at 'the notorious old man', went in a second time with Sammy's group after having already accompanied Hawke.

Kruger was just as portrayed in newspapers, Fry said, with his broadcloth frock coat, big head sunk in his shoulders on a short neck, long biblical face, quick cunning eyes, in a frame of patriachal beard. He stayed seated and all the while smoked Boer tobacco in a large crooked calabash.

A young man translated during the interviews, although Fry thought Kruger understood English. When they went in Sammy introduced his group and said cordially, 'Well, Mr Kruger, we hope we find you well. We have come all this way to see you.' Kruger grunted, and made no reply. It was a silent interview, lasting about half an hour, relieved only by the sweet coffee. Sammy, once outside, remarked that 'the old blighter was not very hearty'. Hawke had been hardly more fortunate in his earlier interview: Kruger had also grunted, and had said only three words.

On to Pietermaritzburg, which was something like a cantonment town in India. It was a British Army station housing a cavalry depot of the 7th Hussars. A drawn cricket match there against a local 15 was notable for the first of two centuries scored off the tourists by a Major Poore, who was quartered there. Robert Montagu Poore, an eccentric giant of a man, who later rose to brigadier, impressed Sammy, even though he did not do so well playing for South Africa in the three Tests. Three years later, appearing in the Hampshire team, Poore headed the English batting figures with an average of over 90. His innings included 304 off Somerset at Taunton, though Sammy missed this match.

A diversion was a polo-hockey match between four mounted Hussars and six of the cricketers, who were on foot and used their sticks cut short like hockey sticks. Sammy and Co. won. But later, back in Johannesburg, they made the mistake of challenging the local polo club at the same game for £100. Not only were they badly beaten, but the riders were less skilled, or more unscrupulous, and, unlike at Pietermaritzburg, allowed their ponies to knock down the English foot men. Hawke stopped the game, probably fearing injuries.

There was plenty of hospitality during the tour, and, wrote Sammy: 'Everywhere we went we had a great reception' (forgetting Kruger). While in Pietermaritzburg the party found themselves dining with the Hussars one evening on which they had also been invited to a smoking concert by the local reception committee. As a result they arrived very late at the concert, but Sammy put things right by his great success on the platform. He could beat Albert Chevalier with his rendering of 'My Old Dutch', Fry thought. Once Sammy was on a platform the question was whether he would ever come off. Fry said he never remembered a less self-conscious performer, nor one who so enjoyed his own interminable repertoire.

Fry also gave an engaging picture of Sammy, with his 'wonderfully persuasive ways . . . his soft voice, confiding smiles, and decisive chin'. On overseas tours with Lord Hawke, his innocent enquiry, 'Who's coming in first with me, Martin?' was as much an institution as the toss.

There were several more matches and a good deal of travelling by train and Cape cart before the first Test at Port Elizabeth on February 15. It resulted in an easy win by 288 runs for England, with Sammy top scorer in the match with 53 in the second innings. He did not bowl, and indeed Lohmann dismissed the home eleven almost single-handed, taking 15 wickets, including the incredible second-innings figure of 8 for 7 in 9.4 overs, when the South Africans were all out for 30.

More tedious travelling (altogether they covered some 3,000 miles in South Africa in the three months) and a couple more matches at Bloemfontein and Pretoria before the second Test in Johannesburg. This ended in another big win, by an innings and 197 runs, after Hawke's men had compiled 482. This time Sammy was one of the opening bowlers, taking a wicket in each innings; but again the hero was Lohmann, who took 9 for 28 in the first innings and was probably robbed of all 10 only by Sammy having dismissed an opener.

A story has come down from this tour of a bowler giving a batsman out – the bowler, of course, being Sammy. The umpire (his name proves elusive) was an English professional coach, more used himself to bowling rather than umpiring. When an express delivery from Sammy brushed the batsman's gloves and was caught by the wicketkeeper, the umpire forgot himself and called out, 'Owzat?' At once Sammy responded: 'Out!' and the batsman departed.

Sammy was involved in one or two amusing but hazardous

incidents during the tour. Once he persuaded Fry to climb through a wire fence round a large compound and pull out one of the luxuriant white tail feathers of a black cock ostrich about 100 yards inside. It ended with Fry fleeing for his life as the ostrich chased him while Sammy pretended to offer the bird a bun.

At a zoo the same two were with a one-time Gloucester player, Howard Francis, a diminutive man who settled in South Africa and later played for his new country. Francis climbed on to the gate of a compound and teased a truculent wildbeeste, which charged the gate. He would have fallen on the animal but for being caught by his coat tail by Fry and then being rescued by Sammy grasping him by the seat of his trousers and recovering him, 'laughing as only Sammy Woods could laugh', said Fry.

After their match at Kimberley Sammy and a few others were invited out to shoot deer. Fry's horse ran away with him, threw him, and a broken ankle ended his cricket on that tour. The others separated into pairs and Sammy said that after a time bullets were whistling round him from Heseltine and Hill. 'Let's fire a few in their direction' said Sammy to his companion, and did so. 'It silenced them for a bit' he recalled.

Sammy hit half-centuries in a couple of matches before the final fixture, the third Test in Cape Town. This again resulted in an innings victory for Hawke's team. In the absence of Fry Sammy moved a place up the batting order to No. 5 and scored 30 in England's total of 265, nearly half of which came from Hayward. Bowling in South Africa's second innings, Sammy had his best Test figures: 3 for 28 in 13 overs.

In the tour as a whole he had a batting average of just over 20 in 28 innings, usually going in at No. 6, but opening two or three times; and had 26 wickets for just over 11 runs apiece.

'I think our trip did a tremendous lot of good,' was his verdict. Later he observed how some of the South African batsmen were to model their style on that of some of the English players.

And so, before he was out of his twenties, ended Sammy's Test career. In the three South African encounters he took 5 wickets for 129, just under 26 apiece. The bowling was dominated by Lohmann, who took 35 wickets for 201 runs in the three matches, and in fact only one other bowler than Sammy took as many as five. In his batting Sammy's total was 122 runs in four innings.

Taking his Test career as a whole, three matches each for his native and his adopted countries, Sammy's record was:

Batting: 10 innings, 154 runs, average 15.40; highest score 53.
Bowling: 412 balls, 10 wickets, average 25.
Catches: 5.

It was not an impressive record, and one is left wondering what he might have achieved if he had played in more Tests when he was bowling at his best. It was a case of being in the wrong place at the wrong time. His early call-up for Australia came when he was in his first year at Cambridge, with virtually no first-class experience and when Ferris and Turner were bowling so well they needed little help. His Tests for England came when he was past his best as a bowler and yet to reach his peak as a batsman. Had he returned to Australia immediately after Cambridge, he may have found a regular place in the Australian team. Had he not already played for Australia he might have found an earlier place in the England XI.

There were some who felt Sammy deserved a place in an England tour of Australia, particularly in 1897–98. England, captained then by both Stoddart and MacLaren, lost the last four of the five Tests, and the omission from the party of Abel, Woods, and Jephson in particular drew comment.

Then, three years after that, it was only a Turkish bath that prevented Sammy from playing in another Test, between Australia and England. This time it would have been against his native country. It happened in February 1901 when MacLaren was leading the team. Sydney Barnes, then a little-known bowler, had shown his artistry in the first two Tests, in which he took 19 wickets, but broke down in the third, and took no further part in the series. At the time Sammy was on a visit to his family in Manly, and helped out by playing for England in one or two minor up-country matches.

When the team for the fourth Test was being selected, it was decided to call him up in place of Barnes, although by now Sammy was known as a batsman and only occasionally successful with the ball. Nonetheless, in a very brief reference in his reminiscences, he said he was to have played 'as the fast bowler'.

The Australians gave MacLaren leave to play him. Sammy's account of why he failed to take part in the Test was simple: 'I had a Turkish bath the night before the game and had to cry off.' It has even been suggested that it might have been a 'diplomatic chill'. That is difficult to believe: Sammy needed no persuasion to play cricket any time, anywhere, with anyone, and the prospect of playing in his native city on the great Sydney ground would seem to have been of overwhelming appeal. Perhaps it was that the rheumatism to which he had become a sufferer was affected too much by the bath. Whatever the truth, he missed the opportunity of having played both for Australia in England and for England in Australia – something achieved by only one man, Billy Midwinter, who managed it while Sammy was still at school.

But if there were no more Tests after South Africa, Sammy still had two more overseas tours ahead: first to the West Indies and then another trip to North America.

The winter of 1896–97 saw not one but two English teams sailing to the West Indies, the one led by Lord Hawke and the other by Arthur Priestley. That there were two parties was all due to a mis-understanding, and some strong words passed between the two captains. Hawke was intolerant of a rival tour. He told Priestley to abandon his, offering in return a place for him in his own team, something Priestley would not otherwise have had on his cricketing ability. Priestley was willing to some extent: he would give up the captaincy, but wanted those he had himself already invited to be included in the party. However, Hawke insisted absolutely on choosing the players he took.

The two men were now on not very good terms. When, once or twice, paths crossed during their tours, they kept angrily aloof from each other, unlike their players, who fraternised happily (not least Sammy). The West Indies were the least wealthy of all the colonies which played cricket, and entertaining two teams was a heavy tax; but they rose admirably to the occasion.

Sammy was in Priestley's party of 13, all amateurs and more than half of them now-forgotten names who (like Priestley) had little or even no experience of the first-class game. The team relied heavily on Stoddart, Sammy, and his Somerset team-mate Richard Palairet. The latter, although not as talented as his brother Lionel, was a competent batsman who later became a cricket administrator and long after-wards, with Warner, was joint manager of the M.C.C.'s 'Bodyline' tour in Australia. There was also a third Somerset man in the party: Henry Stanley, the 'young squire' of Quantock Lodge, whose inclu-sion may have been at Sammy's suggestion.

'We had a most enjoyable time,' Sammy remembered, 'but were badly beaten several times.' Sammy's own performance did not help, since he suffered bad rheumatism from the start of the tour and described himself as 'really a passenger'. He blamed it on a shower he had after practice on the first morning after arriving in Barbardos.

The rheumatism affected his shoulders and neck, and he described himself as 'merely a roundarm bowler' for the whole tour. Nonetheless he was the third most successful bowler, with 35 wickets at 14.31 in the nine major matches, and his batting suffered more, averaging under 14. The tourists lost five of these matches, including one at Port of Spain against All West Indies.

This was the very first match between an English team and one representing all the West Indian islands. The West Indies won by three wickets, the scores being: Mr Priestley's X1 179 and 176, All West Indies 215 and 142 for 7. The most successful English batsman was Palairet, who scored 45 and 46. He opened with his county team-mate Stanley. Top scorer for the West Indies, with 75 not out, was Harold Austin, later to be knighted, who captained the first two West Indian first-class tours of England. Lebrun Constantine, father of the great all-rounder Learie, hit 38 and 45. Three bowlers in the match each took nine wickets – Stoddart and, for the home side, Clifford Goodman and B. Cumberbatch, one white, one black, and the latter a professional. Sammy's contribution was merely useful – batting at No 5 he scored 19 and 26, and his bowling aggregate was 3 for 78.

There was a third outstanding West Indian bowler who did not play in this historic match. His name was Woods, he came from Trinidad, and, like Cumberbatch, he was a black professional. Teams then were virtually all-white, but players of the calibre of Cumberbatch and Woods – both good enough for any English county team, according to Warner – could not be ignored.

In his reminiscences Sammy says that the Woods from Trinidad 'named himself after me'; at first a puzzling remark, since Woods had been called so for some time. However, records up to this time refer to him as 'J. Woods' and afterwards as 'S. Woods', so it would seem he adopted Sammy's first name.

This other S. Woods was described by Warner as 'quite unplayable'. He bowled very fast with a rather low and slinging delivery after approaching the wicket with only two or three paces. He was the bowling success of the West Indies' first tour of England, and took a lot of wickets in the matches against the counties which, however, were not designated as first-class fixtures.

The tour did not include a match against Sammy's county, the nearest fixture being at Bristol against Gloucester. There the negro took a lot of punishment from Jessop and pleaded with his captain to be allowed to take his boots off, as he preferred bowling bare-footed. He so abhorred bowling in boots that, it was said, he more than once secretly removed the soles and played with the uppers little more than spats.

This other Woods played a big part in Trinidad's eight-wicket defeat of Priestley's men at Port of Spain at the end of February, taking altogether 11 wickets for 115 runs. It was the Trinidad team's second victory over the tourists.

For Sammy it was, apart from his rheumatism, another enjoyable tour, and particularly in Jamaica. The party stayed at St. Anne's Bay where, alas, there was no one at the hotel who could mix cocktails – 'a most essential drink in that country to make one alive before breakfast and before dinner', he felt. So Sammy stepped into the breach and made the cocktails before breakfast each day. On one occasion, he joked, the team had to ask for substitutes for the morning's play for two who did not feel so good.

In spite of, or perhaps helped by, Sammy's cocktails (Little Reds and Little Greens they were called), Priestley's team easily won their three matches against Jamaica, plus a couple of minor matches while on the island. In one innings against Jamaica Sammy overcame his rheumatism and took five wickets.

As always Sammy liked socialising, and there were dances with plenty of fun, and also other invitations. But he also just occasionally liked more gentle pursuits. In what he called the Valley of Ferns in Jamaica he went collecting some 50 varieties, golden silver, and stuck them in a book. They were 'still beautiful' when he looked at them many years later.

On another occasion he went fishing in a lake and caught 'a beastly black fish', which he gave to a West Indian. 'Splendid, Stoddy', the man said, and Sammy had to reply, 'I am not Stoddy.' Stoddy, or Stoddart, was on everyone's lips all over the islands. Sammy said that if a horse ran away with a cart the natives would shout out at once, 'Steady, Stoddart, steady!' When Stoddart was batting at Barbados they would beat on the galvanised palings surrounding the ground after he had hit a couple of fours, and shout, 'Steady, Stoddart!'

Stoddart was undoubtedly the hero of the tour, and without him the tourists' playing record would have been less creditable. Of their 16 matches at all levels, they won 10, lost five, and drew the other. Stoddart topped batting and bowling, getting in all matches more than 1,000 runs and over 100 wickets.

Sammy's last overseas tour was in the autumn of 1899, as a member of Ranjitsinhji's team which spent just a month in North America. The Australians should have been the visitors, but disappointed the Philadelphians, and Ranji was invited to take a side. Although all amateurs, the party was far too strong for the opposition, most of them being Test players at some time. The Philadelphians were soundly beaten in their two fixtures, as was Canada in the final match in Toronto. Two other fixtures were drawn.

Apart from Ranji and Sammy, the team included Stoddart, MacLaren, and Jessop. The latter was not a good sailor and 'the smell of Sam Woods' cigars' at every breakfast time he found trying, to say the least. The party also included a young medium-fast bowler named B.J.T. Bosanquet, who was still at Oxford. In between the fall of wickets he demonstrated to his fellow players the 'googly', and Sammy and the rest were greatly interested. Stoddart prophesied that it would prove a success, although it was not for another year or two that Bosanquet began to use his googly, or 'bosie', in matches.

Sammy's contribution to the cricket was negligible. For Somerset that season he had averaged over 40 with the bat, but in North America he totalled 48 runs altogether – which, he pointed out quite happily at a farewell banquet in Philadelphia, 'worked out at .0012 runs per mile'. He took just 13 wickets. 'I didn't enjoy the cricket – it was too one-sided,' he said. Some of the others probably felt the same, for there was a listless look to their fielding.

The social side was another matter. 'We had a most delightful trip as far as pleasure was concerned,' Sammy said. The hospitality was overwhelming at times. The Americans were much excited at the chance to entertain Ranji (a real Prince!), and there was a smell of snobbery about things at times. The *American Cricketer* made the point that all the party were 'college men and the social equals of the Prince'. They were all lavishly kitted out with clothing and equipment in the Prince's own Nawanagar team colours.

But there was an unpleasant incident in Philadelphia involving Gilbert Jessop. Some friends took him to the negro quarters to see the 'hootchy-kootchy'. It was an erotic dance and Jessop disapproved of what he saw. He made the mistake of saying so, and was advised to leave promptly. As he opened the door there was a plunk on the panel just above his head, and he saw a cut-throat razor embedded there. It is not recorded if Sammy was with him on this occasion. Perhaps not, as otherwise there would most likely have been further developments.

There was another visit for Sammy to the Niagara Falls, and an invitation from the grocery magnate, Sir Thomas Lipton, to go aboard his steam yacht, the *Erin*, to watch his racing yacht *Shamrock* take part in the America's Cup. His hospitality was lavish, but the weather spoiled the racing that day.

The tour was marred by only a few mishaps. There was a minor train collision, in which a sleeping MacLaren was deposited on the floor, and several misadventures with the baggage which actually delayed the start of a couple of matches. For Victor Barton, ex-soldier and Hampshire professional, who was taken along as baggage master, life was full of headaches.

The journey home was the maiden voyage from America of the *Oceania*, and the weather was fine, although one or two of the cricketers, notably Ranji and Jessop, would still have preferred to be on dry land. A day or two out from England news was signalled from outgoing vessels they passed that Kruger had declared war. The news was received with derision by most of the cricketers.

Sammy was to learn a few months later that his friend, Henry Stanley, of Quantock Lodge, who had been to the West Indies with him, was dead. He had been killed, at the age of 27, in a skirmish with the Boers. Sammy's own brother, Harris, who had returned to New South Wales after his education in England, also fought in the Boer War, serving with the cavalry and returning safely afterwards to Australia.

'Playing with the Swells'

Sammy was 21 and in his freshman's year at Cambridge when he was selected to play for the Gentlemen against the Players; or, as he put it, when he first 'played with the swells'. It was as important a fixture as a Test match in those days. Even 30 years later Warner could write that it was still the ambition of every cricketer, amateur or professional, to appear in this contest – 'an honour, setting, as it were, a hallmark on a player's career'.

The fixture dated back to 1806 and for the first half-century or so the Players – the professionals – had dominated. The arrival of W.G. Grace, who first played for the Gentlemen while still only 16, changed the balance.

During the years Sammy appeared, the Gentlemen and Players met three and sometimes four times a year: at Lord's and the Oval in July and at Scarborough or Hastings, or both, in September.

Sammy arrived in sensational fashion, provided several remarkable bowling performances in the following years, and ended captaining the side in 1900 and leading the Gentlemen to a dramatic defeat which brought both criticism and praise for his decisions in the match.

At Lord's on the morning of July 9, 1888, Sammy and another new bowler in the team, Aubrey Smith, the future Hollywood actor, with whom he had played on his first-class debut two years before, found themselves in a team alongside half-a-dozen Test players. The professionals, too, had not a little Test experience in their ranks. Neither of the newcomers seems to have been overawed, however, and each produced a performance which played a big part in the Gentlemen's five-run victory.

The Players were led by George Ulyett, for whom Sammy, as a 14-year-old in Sydney, had once bought a drink and bowled to at the nets. It was a difficult wicket, and only one player in the match, W.G. Grace, reached double figures in both innings. The Gentlemen, put in to bat by Ulyett, were all back in the pavilion that afternoon for 84. The Players could manage a lead of only 23, with Sammy and Smith, who opened the bowling together, taking five and three wickets

The Taunton ground in Sammy's day.

The 1901 Somerset team which scored that incredible win over Yorkshire: *left to right, back row* –
G.C. Gill, E. Robson, L.C. Braund, G. Burrington; *centre* – F.A. Phillips, A.E. Newton, Sammy
Woods, L.C.H. Palairet, V.T. Hill; *front* – B. Cranfield, A.E. Lewis.

Yorkshire v. Somerset,

At Headingley, Leeds, July 15, 16, and 17, 1901.

Umpires :—Messrs. W. Wright & T. Mycroft. Draw at 6-30

SOMERSET.

1	L. C. H. Palairet b Hirst	o	c & b Brown ...	173
2	Braund b Rhodes... ...	o	b Haigh ...	107
3	Lewis c Tunnicliffe b Rhodes	10	b Rhodes ...	12
4	F. A. Phillips b Hirst	12	b Wainwright ...	122
5	S. M. J. Woods c Hunter b Haigh	46	c Tunnicliffe b Hirst	66
6	V. T. Hill run out	o	c Hirst b Rhodes	53
7	Robson c Hunter b Rhodes	o	c Tunnicliffe b Rhodes	40
8	Gill ... c Hunter b Rhodes	4	stp. Hunter b Rhodes	14
9	A. E. Newton b Haigh	o	c Taylor b Rhodes	4
10	G. Burrington c Brown b Rhodes	11	stp. Hunter b Rhodes	15
11	Cranfield not out ...	1	not out ...	5
	Extras	3	Extras	19
	Total	87	Total	630

Total Runs at the fall of each wicket.

o o 16 32 38 38 64 65 86 l 222 244 341 466 522 570 597 604 609

Bowling.	Overs.	Maidens.	Runs.	Wickets.	Overs.	Maidens.	Runs.	Wickets
Hirst ...	12	5	36	2	37	1	189	1
Rhodes ...	16	8	39	5	46.5	12	145	6
Haigh ...	4	0	9	2	20	4	78	1
Wainwright	...	...	...	...	34	3	107	1
Brown ...					18	1	92	1

Hirst, 3 n balls

NEW INN, Best Refreshments, Largest and Best Rooms in Headingley.

YORKSHIRE.

1	Brown c Braund b Cranfield	24	c Sub b Gill ...	5
2	Tunnicliffe c Newton b Gill ...	9	c Palairet b Braund	44
3	Denton c Woods b Gill ...	12	b Braund ...	16
4	T. L. Taylor b Cranfield ...	1	retired, hurt ...	o
5	F. Mitchell b Gill ...	4	b Braund ...	21
6	Hirst c Robson b Cranfield	61	lbw b Braund ..	6
7	Wainwright b Gill	9	c Lewis b Cranfield	1
8	Lord Hawke b Robson ...	37	c Burrington b Cranfield	4
9	Haigh c Robson b Cranfield	96	not out ...	2
10	Rhodes c Lewis b Robson ...	44	stp Newton b Cranfield	o
11	Hunter not out	10	c Woods b Cranfield	o
	Extras	18	Extras	14
	Total	325	Total	113

Total Runs at the fall of each wicket.

13 33 44 51 55 86 142 167 285 14 57 91 99 104 109 109 109

Bowling.	Overs.	Maidens.	Runs.	Wickets.	Overs.	Maidens.	Runs.	Wickets
Cranfield	27	5	113	4	5 w's 18	5	35	4
Gill ...	23	2	105	4	4	1	23	1
Braund ...	5	0	33	0	15	3	41	4
Robson ...	10	1	35	2	...	...	...	...
Woods ...	5	1	21	0				
Palairet ...	1	1	o	0				

'Oh Woods-man, spare that tree,' pleads the Yorkshire captain, Lord Hawke, in this *Athletic News* cartoon at the time of Somerset's remarkable victories over the champion county.

Sammy was a favourite of the cartoonists: this one by 'Rip' is from the early years of the century.

A bowler's view of Sammy in his heyday.

A light-hearted moment at Khartoum in 1916.

The presentation of a testimonial cheque to Sammy in an interval of Yorkshire's match at Taunton in 1907.

E. Robson (1895–1923).

L.C. Braund (1899–1920).

Two Somerset cricket captains who also captained England at rugby: John Daniell (left) and Sammy.

One of his last innings: Sammy goes out to bat in a village match at Broadway, in south Somerset.

respectively. In the second innings the Gentlemen fared little better than in their first knock, being all out for exactly 100, leaving the Players to make 78 to win.

It looked all over when they had reached 71 with four wickets left, but then Allan Steel, the Gentlemen's captain, brought Smith back to join Sammy. They shared the remaining wickets with only one run being added. Sammy's figures for the match were 10 for 76 in 46.2 overs. Seven were bowled, including in both innings Ulyett, then regarded as the best batsman Yorkshire had produced and a veteran of over 20 Tests. Other victims whose stumps he hit included Bobby Abel. The Lord's crowd gave Sammy 'a great reception', he remembered. Smith could be no less pleased with his debut, having a match aggregate of 5 for 36.

In a few days the Players had their revenge at the Oval. The Gentlemen, who had by far the worst of a rain-affected wicket, lost by an innings in another low-scoring match. But again Sammy distinguished himself, altogether taking 5 wickets for 58 and again bowling both Ulyett and Abel.

Sammy's debut for the Gentlemen of England was followed quickly by his appearance in his first Test for Australia – a fact which provided a peg for a jingoistic passage from the chairman, H. Smith Wright M.P., at the Old Brightonians' dinner. The college magazine reported:

> He thought that formed a sort of golden link in the imperial chain which bound us to our colonies, and the name of Woods would be remembered in that connection as long as Brighton College should last. Our national sports were indeed one of the great connecting links between us and our Colonies. These sports seemed to be the one feature which distinguished us from all other nations on the earth. Germany and France could not colonise much because they had no cricket or football. . . .

In his four matches for the Gentlemen in the following two years Sammy was less impressive, managing only nine wickets altogether. But he was back in match-winning form at the Oval in 1891 with his fellow Australian Ferris, who was at the time qualifying to play for Gloucester. The Gentlemen won this encounter by an innings and 54 runs, the Players being caught on a drying pitch in their second knock. A sponge was used to dry the wicket after rain on the second day.

Sammy took six wickets in the first innings and in the second three (9–96). Ferris took 7 for 28 in the second innings, when the Players were dismissed for 59. The rain returned to spoil the Lord's match three days later.

It was in his only appearance in the fixture at Hastings, in September 1892, that Sammy was to produce one of his best bowling performances of 16 appearances for the Gentlemen. After his team had scored 211, the professionals were sent back for 109, with Sammy taking 8 for 46. One was run out and the other wicket fell to Stoddart, who, it is recorded, drank Sammy's health when they dined that evening, saying, 'Well bowled, we two!'

Required to bat again, the Players amassed 388 before declaring with three wickets left. The limitations of the Gentlemen's attack had been exposed when Grace strained his knee early on. Sammy, ever a willing horse, bowled no fewer than 65 overs (of five balls) in this innings; but he took only three wickets and had 201 runs scored off him. In the end the Gentlemen had to struggle to save the match.

Sammy's next appearance for the Gentlemen was in July 1894 at Lord's, which will be remembered for the feat of bowling unchanged in both innings with his fellow Cambridge Blue, Jackson. The Gentlemen won by an innings after having batted first on a slow pitch and scored a comparatively modest 254, mainly due to half-centuries by Grace and Jackson. Sammy recorded his biggest score so far for the Gentlemen: batting at No. 10 he was 27 not out when his old friend MacGregor was dismissed.

The weather this time favoured the Gentlemen. At the end of the first day the Players had lost four men for 49 on a fast-drying pitch before poor light stopped play, to be followed by rain. Next day, with Sammy and Jackson bowling well, the latter the more economical, the innings closed at 108. In the second innings the same bowlers continued to dominate, with Jackson outshining Sammy. MacGregor was in fine form behind the stumps, and aided by some good fielding, the Players were dismissed this time for 107. Whereas the Players had called on seven bowlers, the Gentlemen had used just the two. Their figures were:

		Overs	Maidens	Runs	Wickets
1st innings	Woods	24.2	8	61	4
	Jackson	24	8	36	5
2nd innings	Woods	21.4	6	63	2
	Jackson	21	7	41	7

The last time two bowlers had bowled unchanged in a Gentlemen v. Players contest had been 15 years before, and it was never to happen again.

Sammy happily recalled that

> Jackson had the biggest share in this achievement, for I only got six wickets and he got 12. Briggs and Wainwright [Lancashire and Yorkshire respectively and both Test players] in the second innings made a stand. I remember the 'old man' [W.G. Grace] saying to me 'I think I will have a bowl now'. I said, 'I don't think so yet', and although I didn't separate them Jackson did.

The M.C.C. committee presented Sammy and Jackson with a trophy in the shape of a ball mounted in silver and alabaster.

Sammy, his bowling on the wane, appeared only once in the next three seasons. In 1896 he contributed to the Gentlemen's victory with seven wickets. But in 1898 he was recalled for what was a very special occasion: a match coinciding with Grace's 50th birthday, for which two very strong sides were selected.

It was just ten years since Sammy had first played for the Gentlemen. Then he had been a bowler; now he was a batsman, though he said he did not know why he was chosen instead of his fellow Somerset player Lionel Palairet. 'I suppose it was because it was W.G.'s 50th birthday and the committee wanted as many captains as possible,' he thought. 'Still, I got 6 wickets and a few runs. We had all the worst of the wicket, and lost close on time.'

Sammy was doubtless right about the committee's selection policy, and there was some criticism at the time of players like Palairet and Jessop (not yet Gloucester's captain) being omitted. Not only were most of Grace's team county captains, most also played for England, and indeed four captained their country. Nearly all the Players, too, had represented England, and they were led by Arthur Shrewsbury, who captained teams from England on two tours to Australia.

Sammy and Grace were by now, of course, very well known to each other and there was mutual respect. It was about this time that Grace wrote of Sammy that he was 'a giant in size, in strength, and in pluck'.

There were similarities in character as well as in physique between the two men, as several contemporaries noted. The 'ghost' for Grace's book of reminiscences, a journalist called Arthur Porritt, wrote in a volume of his own that Grace was 'a big grown-up boy, just what a man who only lived when he was in the open might be expected to be.' And one of Grace's biographers quotes a friend of the great man as saying he was 'just a great big schoolboy in everything he did'. They both might have been referring to Sammy. As might that same biographer, Bernard Darwin, when he wrote of Grace's schoolboy love for elementary and boisterous jokes, distaste for learning, and his undisguised keenness.

Sammy's friendship and respect for Grace's unrivalled achievements did not blind him to his gamesmanship. One biographer has put it that Grace was 'so passionately committed to the game that he pushed the parameters of fair play beyond legitimate bounds'. Sammy neatly summed it up more concisely. Grace, he said, was 'an artful old toad'.

Sammy could get away with saying things that others would not dare. Once when he had comprehensively bowled Grace, he called out, 'I shouldn't go, doctor – there's still one stump standing.'

Another time he was playing under Grace when, after a hard day in the field, they faced 40 minutes of batting in deteriorating light. As Grace was preparing to open as usual, Sammy went to him in the dressing room and said: 'Old man, you are *not* going in tonight.' Grace sharply replied, 'Look here, Sam, who is captain of this side, you or me?' Sammy replied: 'Give yourself a chance, you are not so young as you were, and tired out too. Let someone else go in first and reserve yourself for tomorrow.' Grace stared at him in silence for a moment, then said: 'All right, Sam, write down the batting order.' Next day Grace went in lower in the order and hit a half-century.

The author of a column in the *Western Daily Press*, signed by the initials 'A.G.P.', recalled in a tribute to Sammy after his death that there were occasions when their wills clashed. 'Indeed,' he wrote, 'I always thought that these two giants of the game preserved a sort of armed neutrality.'

As it happened, just two months before this Gentlemen v. Players match of 1898 the two had a more public and less happy exchange of opinion. It happened in what was always a very keenly fought fixture, that between Somerset and Gloucester. ('What a sight it was,' one who often saw it remembered, 'to see W.G. Grace and S.M.J. Woods out in front of the pavilion tossing for innings.') One of the Gloucester batsmen, Harry Wrathall, a professional, was handicapped in running. Another professional, Jack Board, came out to run for him. Now Board, who was about the fastest man in the side, was not wearing pads, and Sammy soon realised that as a result Gloucester were gaining a run or two.

Sammy therefore asked Board to put on pads. Grace objected to the request. The upshot was that Grace told Board to leave the field and Wrathall had to run himself – 'a case of cutting off your nose to spite yourself', as one paper commented.

But all was harmony again before the Gentlemen's match (the likelihood was, indeed, that they had a drink or two together that very evening). Years later Gloucester honoured their old adversary by making Sammy a life member of the club.

This was Grace's penultimate appearance for the Gentlemen at Lord's, although he continued to play for them in matches at other venues until 1906, when he finally bid farewell.

Excursion trains ran from the West for the great occasion, Grace's 50th birthday, which was blessed with fine weather, apart from an hour's rain on the second day. When Grace led the Gentlemen on the field at the start on Monday, July 18, he met with a great welcome. Over 17,000 people had paid for admission that day, and they joined with members in the pavilion in standing up and waving their hats in the air and shouting their appreciation.

For the first time a cinematograph operator was at Lord's to shoot a film there. What survives is a short piece showing the two teams, the amateurs and the professionals, walking on the field in pairs. The only conversation that can be observed, though not heard, is Sammy saying something to Lilley – without taking from his lips a cigarette from which he was puffing clouds of smoke.

Sammy was, of course, no longer opening bowler. Kortright, one of the fastest of all, and Jackson launched the attack, followed by Townsend and Grace himself. Only then did Sammy take the ball. As it happened, he proved the most successful in terms of wickets: he took three in each innings for a total of 111 runs. His wickets included the prize one of Shrewsbury, who was making his last appearance for the Players, and with his slower ball he bowled all over his wicket Billy Gunn, the Nottingham giant, who had made a century. When he went out to bat, at No. 8, Sammy got his usual great reception. Although he faced only a few balls he hit one into the pavilion before being bowled on 13. In the second innings he scored nine.

It proved a suitably exciting match. Thanks mainly to two fine innings by Gunn, with 139 and 56, and able support from William Storer (the Derbyshire wicketkeeper, being played on this occasion for his batting alone), whose two contributions totalled 132, the Gentlemen were set 296 to win. On a wicket which had deteriorated after rain, they were soon in trouble. Despite a valiant effort by Grace, batting low in the order because of a damaged hand, they lost by 137 runs. Jack Hearne, who bowled Sammy in both innings, was the bowling hero, taking 11 wickets.

The single occasion when Sammy was to captain the Gentlemen, in 1900, provided what *Wisden* judged to be 'the most remarkable game of the whole season'. There were some memorable individual performances, an unexpected result, and also controversy. Again there were two strong teams, the Players now being captained by Abel.

The match, which began on July 16, at Lord's, and was played in oppressive heat, was notable in that for the first time in 35 years, Grace was not on the field. The greatest of the individual triumphs was that of Reginald ('Tip') Foster, just 22 and playing for both Oxford and Worcester that year. He took almost half an hour to score his first run, and then hit a century; the first time a Gentleman had managed this on his debut in the fixture. Then he scored another in the second innings. Fry, overshadowed by the newcomer, hit 68 and the innings closed on 297 (of which Sammy provided just the seven). The Players were all out for 136 the next morning, Sammy using five bowlers but not himself.

Sammy decided not to enforce the follow on. There was the second century from Foster, with whom Fry shared a third-wicket partnership of nearly 200, and the Gentlemen were in what seemed an impregnable position.

With a lead of 400 and seven wickets in hand, Sammy gave the order for his batsmen to hit out so that his bowlers could have a go at the Players late in the day. Runs came quickly, and wickets fell too. Sammy recorded a duck, caught first ball at long leg. Jessop, who was told by the captain he had 'five minutes', hit 18 off the only six balls he received. The innings closed on 339, leaving the Players to get 501 to win.

The Gentlemen claimed a valuable wicket before stumps were drawn, that of the Lancashire opener, Albert Ward. But the next day Abel hit 98 and centuries came from J.T. Brown, of Yorkshire, and Hayward; and what had seemed an impossible target gradually came within reach.

When young Wilfred Rhodes, then at the start of his long career with Yorkshire, came in at the fall of the eighth wicket, the score was 485. Fifteen runs were added, and the scores were level as the clock reached 6.30.

But it was not to be a draw. Sammy never liked draws ('no good except for bathing', as he said), and quickly took the ball. So far in the innings he had claimed one wicket for nearly 70 runs; but now perhaps he hoped he could dismiss the last two and make it a tie. Alas for him, off the fifth ball of the over Rhodes made the winning hit, the batsmen ran two (why? they needed only one) and the Players had won by two wickets.

Sammy, inevitably, came in for criticism on two counts. Lilley, the Players' wicketkeeper, called that extra over after time an act of generous sportsmanship on Sammy's part, 'so characteristic of him'. But others saw it differently. 'Plum' Warner, who probably would have played in the match but for injury, was present and later wrote an account in which he said: 'That extra over was too magnanimous and the rule as to the time fixed for the drawing of stumps was broken, and what were the umpires about?' The M.C.C. committee, when they met, viewed Sammy's extra over with disfavour. After all, rules were rules.

But the main criticism of Sammy was of his tactic in ordering his players to hit out or get out in the second afternoon. The author of the lengthy report of the match in *Wisden* seemed to have been peeved by the fact that the Gentlemen lost. He wrote that some people went so far as to say that if the Gentlemen could not win with a lead of 500 runs, they did not deserve to win at all; and went on:

> This was all very well, but the fact remained that there was only one possible way by which the Gentlemen could lose the match, and that their captain adopted it. If he had not been so anxious for his side to be out before the end of the second afternoon he could have made defeat absolutely impossible, and yet have left his side a whole day to win.

However, the writer concluded, although the Gentlemen suffered a defeat that was unnecessary, the public profited as the cricket on the last day was 'quite a marvel of sustained interest'.

The *Athletic News* took a more positive view. It described Sammy as 'a thorough-going sportsman' and went on to say that 'whilst he might have allowed his men to pile on runs and thus make defeat impossible, he preferred to make a dash for victory . . . He certainly gave the cue to a sensational finish.'

Of that extra over, it merely observed: 'To arrive at a conclusion play was continued beyond the time for drawing.'

Warner, in his account, was somewhat critical of the way Sammy handled his strong bowling attack in the second innings (though not in the first!): 'The great heat no doubt made the management of fast bowling of some difficulty, but Woods' captaincy was on this occasion not up to his usual standard,' he said.

In his reminiscences, Sammy was unrepentant. Of his final over, he wrote simply that 'I had an over after time and they got them [the runs]'. Of his tactics on the second afternoon, he said:

> Well, had I left my side to bat until time on the second day and not have given the Players a chance of getting the runs, a pretty nice day's play would have resulted. Our present Somerset captain [John Daniell] is very often doing the same thing, and all I wish is that there were more captains like him playing at present.

Sammy played again for the Gentlemen, at Scarborough at the end of August, when a below-strength side, now captained by Lord Hawke, was beaten by an innings. Batting at No. 7, Sammy hit his highest score in his appearances for the Gentlemen, 52; and claimed three wickets. His final match for them was also at Scarborough, in 1902, when he took just one wicket.

Sammy particularly enjoyed Scarborough – 'delightful times', he said, and: 'Short hours on account of the dew or sea mist. Keennest and friendliest of cricket. Lots of good "lotion" and lovely air. A good tonic to finish up with after a hard summer's work.' And there could not be, he felt, 'a more sporting crowd of holiday spectators than those who attend there.'

One story about Sammy during a Scarborough festival concerns the time he shared a room with the rather more serious MacLaren. Sammy announced he was going to a ball on the eve of a match. When MacLaren woke next morning he found his room-mate still in evening dress and starting the day with a half bottle of champagne.

MacLaren gave Sammy a bit of a lecture. Then Sammy went to the match, scored a lot of runs, and took several wickets. MacLaren had a poor day, failing with the bat and dropping catches. Sammy commiserated: 'Too much sleep, old son. Makes a man drowsy.'

His batting in the Gentlemen v. Players series was generally disappointing, although usually he did not go into until No. 9 or 10. His average in 25 innings was only 11.36. His bowling, however, accounted for 75 batsmen at 19.90. Over half of his wickets were claimed without another player being involved: 33 were bowled, one hit wicket, four were caught and bowled, and two were lbw.

As Warner wrote, in many matches, particularly the earlier ones, Sammy carried the Gentlemen's bowling. Apart from the occasion at the Oval when he and Jackson bowled unchanged, there was an earlier match in which Sammy bowled without a rest from 11.30 until 5.30. Grace, said Warner, 'has no compunctions at working his best bowler, especially when he was as strong as Sammy was.'

There were also other, less important, appearances for teams representing the Gentlemen of England. One of these provided an example of Sammy's kindly attitude to cricketers not much younger than himself. It was recalled by G.O. Smith, Oxford cricket and soccer Blue. (Later 'G.O.' played a few innings for Surrey, but was better known as the best centre-forward of his day.) He had done well in one or two early-season games at Oxford and, not yet a Blue, was given his chance for the university when it entertained a Gentlemen of England team, which included Sammy. As 'G.O.' was going in to bat Sammy, a mere five years his senior, said: 'Young fellow, I think you are nervous'; to which he replied, 'Yes, I am.' Sammy then, in a gruff voice, told him: 'The first two balls you will get from me will be full tossess to leg. If you can't hit them both for four I shall bowl you out.' 'G.O.' got his eight runs off Sammy's gift deliveries, and went on to make a half-century.

Champagne Victory

Sammy was one of the sporting cartoonists' favourites. His determined chin, his shock of hair, his broad smile, his mighty hitting, his shirt hanging out as he steamed in to bowl – all were familiar to newspaper readers who never ventured near a cricket ground. The cartoons partly compensated for the lack of action photographs in those days.

Those that appeared in the early years of this century sometimes featured him with Lord Hawke. One shows Sammy standing near a tree labelled 'White Rose', while Hawke, on bended knee, is praying, 'Oh Woods-man spare that tree'. Another shows him holding Hawke down in a vat of cider, with Sammy saying, 'Better be drowned in Somerset cider than Lancashire beer. It is more soothing.' Yet another shows a jaunty Sammy, striding out in a blazer and straw hat, puffing at a cigar, and wearing in his buttonhole a white rose.

The follower of cricket – and many besides – would have had no difficulty in knowing what they were all about. For one of the sensations of the start of the new century, not once but twice, was lowly Somerset's defeats of the mighty and otherwise unbeaten Yorkshire team. The match of 1901, indeed, must rank still, nearly a century later, as among the most incredible in the history of the county championship for its change in fortune. Sammy's men seemed to be headed for an innings rout and instead inflicted a crushing defeat on the champions.

Yorkshire were the undisputed champions in the opening years of the century. In 1900 they were unbeaten, and in 1901 and 1902 they lost just one game in each season: both to Somerset.

In the first of two encounters in 1901 between the counties at Taunton, Somerset had given the northerners a fright. In a nail-biting finish, Yorkshire had won by one wicket, with only a couple of minutes left.

The return match was at Headingley on Monday, July 15. Not for the first time Sammy had a job making up a team. He won the toss, gambled by batting on a damp pitch, and almost immediately the

106

openers and two best batsmen, Lionel Palairet and Len Braund, were back in the pavilion without a run on the board, victims of the two great Yorkshire bowlers, George Hirst and Wilfred Rhodes.

More wickets fell cheaply (there were five ducks in all), only Sammy himself offering much resistance. Of Somerset's total of 87 he scored 46, and it was only his 'brilliant innings', reported *Cricket*, 'which saved his side from extreme disaster.' Yorkshire then lost early wickets, but at the end of the first day had reached 325, which Sammy felt they should not have done on what proved 'a fiery wicket'. Their pace bowler, Schofield Haigh, batting at No. 9, hit 96, and Hirst and Rhodes together contributed over 100.

That evening Sammy, Palairet, and a couple of other Somerset players had 'a very good dinner' with the Mayor of Leeds. The brandy liqueur was described by their host as 'the best in the land', so Sammy promptly asked for the tiny liqueur glasses to be replaced by claret glasses, which was done. There was some talk of Somerset leaving to return home at the end of the second day: they faced a deficit of 238 and the Mayor did not expect them to last long in the second innings.

Sammy, perhaps by now well into the brandy liqueur, said that the train arrangements would be for the end of Wednesday, the third day, by which time Somerset would have won. Presently the Mayor said that if Somerset won, he would give them £100. 'I never got it,' Sammy said in later years (although he did get £10 out of a match wager, having bet 10 to one that Palairet would score a century).

The next day Palairet and Braund hit 222 for the first wicket in two hours and 20 minutes. Braund survived an appeal for a catch at slip when he was 55. Sammy, from beyond the boundary, could not tell whether the ball hit the ground or not before 'Long John' Tunnicliffe took it. Lord Hawke regarded it as 'the fairest of catches'. Unfortunately one umpire, Tom Mycroft, 'could not see', and the other, Walter Wright, 'gave it against us'. After that, Hawke 'never seemed to get my boys going again.'

Other fielders were as sure as Hawke that it was a catch, and one, Ted Wainwright, never forgot. 'Len Braund were out, reight enough,' he said. 'Walter Wright lost us t' match.' And he was still saying it years later. Hirst was so upset he did not trust himself to speak to Wright, the former Nottingham and Kent bowler, through the afternoon. But when Sammy's men had passed 500, he said as he walked past the umpire, 'Hey, Walter, tha knows tha art a foo-il!'

As well as the openers, Francis Phillips, a schoolmaster, batting at

No. 4, scored a century, Sammy acting as his runner most of his innings as he strained a leg. The bowlers were tiring, especially Hirst, who had been worked hard that season. He told Sammy: 'My feet are so sore I can hardly run up to the wicket.' The Somerset captain himself scored 66 in a breezy innings, hitting all round the wicket; and there were useful contributions from one or two others. When stumps were drawn the scoreboard read 549 for 5. At the close of the innings next morning Somerset had reached 630 – the most that any county scored against Yorkshire until Leicestershire went 51 better in 1996.

It was fast scoring, too. But in spite of their overall lack of success at this period, Somerset were rarely slow run-getters. According to research by Gerald Brodribb covering the years 1895 to 1904, of which he gives the results in his book *All Round the Wicket*, they were in fact the fastest-scoring county of all in that decade.

Yorkshire then surprisingly collapsed, mainly thanks to some fine bowling by Braund, with his leg-breaks, and Beaumont Cranfield, a slow left-armer, who took four wickets apiece. They were helped by some rather better catching than Somerset usually produced in those years. The final wicket fell to a catch by Sammy, who annexed the ball. The champions were out for 113, and Somerset had won by 279 runs.

Back in Taunton crowds had gathered in the town as telegrams arrived telling of Somerset's progress, and excitement grew. At Headingley the crowd of 6,000 took the defeat in good spirit. 'We had a great reception after the game,' Sammy recalled. 'The crowd cheered themselves hoarse.' He maintained long afterwards that there were no greater sportsmen in the world than the Yorkshiremen. When he eventually managed to reach a hansom cab it was several minutes before people would let him leave the ground. At the hotel Sammy strode in and uttered one cogent word: 'Champagne!'

The London *Evening News* had a contents bill out that Wednesday evening given up to a cartoon of the Somerset captain with a big smile on his face and the single word: SAMMY. At Taunton railway station later townsfolk gathered to await the return of the heroes. At King's College, a local public school, the boys were let off prep. to mark the great victory.

Writing of the match long afterwards Lord Hawke said that Somerset were deservedly the heroes and that 'It was absolutely the only occasion during all my captaincy [28 years] when I could not make my side buck up.' However, he also felt it was an occasion when for once Sammy's reputation for sportsmanship suffered a lapse.

According to Hawke, the wicket began to crumble badly at the end of the second day, when Somerset had already complied most of their big score. Next morning Sammy put on the heavy roller to make it worse.

'I remember telling him that I really thought he was a better sportsman,' wrote Hawke, 'for he well knew that we never had "an earthly" to get the runs. I always imagined the roller was to be used to benefit your own side, not to break up the wicket for your opponent.'

The following June saw Yorkshire's only defeat in 1902 in the county championship, this time at Sheffield. In a low-scoring match Somerset triumphed by 34 runs, with Braund the hero with 15 wickets for 71. And in 1903, when Yorkshire slipped to third place in the championship, they were again beaten by Sammy's men, this time at Taunton.

Sammy had again topped 1,000 runs in that season of 1901, but he took only 19 wickets all summer and they cost over 30 runs each. However, one of them was his 1,000th wicket in first-class cricket. Now he became one of the first half-dozen cricketers (Grace, of course, being the first) to achieve the all-rounders' double of 10,000 runs and 1,000 wickets.

Things were looking up just a bit for the team now, especially with the arrival of Braund. In addition to four championship wins they easily defeated the touring South Africans. There were still many long days in the field, though, and the bowlers suffered at the hands of Ranji that summer — in spite of his fishing.

There are several versions of the story, but what it seems happened was that Ranji, who loved fishing, was told that there were plenty of perch to be had in a mill pond not far from the Taunton ground where Sussex were playing. Sammy was not taking part in this match, but he egged on some of the Somerset team to tempt Ranji into going night-fishing.

Now Ranji was a night person who could keep late hours without apparently affecting his cricket. But he was now captain of Sussex and sensitive to the feelings of team-mates. The next day, the last of the match, Sussex needed to make a lot of runs to avoid the risk of defeat. So that night he deposited his boots outside his hotel door and it was assumed he had retired.

Later Ranji crept out, wearing a spare pair of boots, and went fishing — 'the whole night', according to at least one of his bio-graphers. What he caught is not recorded; but Somerset certainly caught it. Ranji took his overnight score of 29 to 285 not out in a faultless innings, and the game ended in a draw. Sammy joked that he could have made it 400 had he not been a bit tired through having a night out!

It was in the same year that Sammy earned a mention in *Punch* for his singing. The author was the creator of Sherlock Holmes, Arthur Conan Doyle, himself playing first-class cricket for the M.C.C. at this time. Very likely his and Sammy's paths crossed.

Doyle's piece was prefaced by a quote from an American financier: 'First-class cricket, properly organised and run as an attractive variety show, would be a fine paying concern.' Doyle then set out a day's programme of non-stop entertainment at Lord's, presented by the Anglo-American Willow-and-Leather Syndicate, featuring famous cricketers. The concluding item was the entire cast singing 'The Star-Spangled Banner', with a solo item by S.M.J. Woods.

Doyle's amusing piece was fiction, but there was a true incident worthy of *Punch* not long before when Sammy turned out for the M.C.C. against Hereford. A military gentleman was in his team, and just before he went out to bat Sammy got behind him and secured a baby's bell to the belt of his trousers. Soon after reaching the wicket, the batsman took a quick single, and as he ran the fielders heard 'Tinkle, tinkle'. The fielding captain asked: 'Is this your usual custom?' Recounting the incident, *Cricket* said that the military gentleman 'smiled, shook his head, but all he ventured to say was "Sammy Woods, Sammy Woods"; but brief as that was it conveyed much.'

Sammy, his cricket, and his pranks were now a legend far beyond the boundaries of Somerset. One of his fans was Arthur Waugh, literary critic and managing director of Chapman and Hall, the firm which later published Sammy's reminiscences. Alec, one of his two novelist sons, recalled an early memory of Waugh returning from a day at Lord's and saying to his wife: 'Would you like to kiss this hand before I wash it. It has shaken hands with Sammy Woods.' The family also treasured an earthenware water jug which bore medallions of Sammy and Gregor MacGregor.

In the early part of 1902 Sammy returned to Australia to see his family, for the first time in almost 20 years. The ship sailed via Cape Town and went as far south as the Kerguelen Islands – 'very cold . . . somewhere near the South Pole, I reckon,' said Sammy. He was, of course, much involved in the fun and games aboard.

Sammy befriended 'a little parson' he called Mike. A fancy-dress parade was arranged to mark the latter's birthday, Sammy dressing as a pierrot. The parson appeared as Charley's Aunt and although, according to Sammy, a teetotaller, ended up flinging nuts at the captain's table. There was also aboard 'a ripping sporting girl' named Brown, who led Sammy and about a score of others playing 'Follow the man from Cook's'. This involved them processing all over the ship, even on the bridge, and into the smoking room where the 'old fossils' were awakened.

Sammy's temperament is illustrated by the story of his reunion with his family as told by Jessop, who was then in Australia as one of MacLaren's England team. Strolling down the gangway, Sammy took a pipe out of his pocket, filled it, and then looked in vain for a match. He approached his father, and friends of the family stood aside, sensible of the importance of the occasion. 'Hello, guv'nor,' said the returning hero. 'Have you got a match?'

Sammy helped out the England team in one or two of their up-country matches, and but for that unfortunate Turkish bath already referred to would have played for them in the fourth Test in Sydney. This would have been because Barnes had injured his knee in the previous Test at Adelaide, and hardly because Sammy had shown any exceptional form in the non-first-class matches in which he played. Following the second Test in Melbourne he turned out twice for the tourists against Stawell District and Ballarat, the home teams in each case playing 18 men; and then before the Adelaide Test he took part in a match against 18 of Western District. In these three games he scored a total of 21 runs (19 from one innings), and bowling in two of them he took just four wickets for 87 runs.

Sammy was delighted when Braund made a century in the third Test. When he went into the dressing room at the end of Braund's innings, he was so proud of the Somerset professional's achievement that he took the pin from his own tie and handed it to him. Braund wore the memento for years to come.

Mike the parson watched the Sydney Test and afterwards Sammy and his brother, 'Stringy Bark', invited him to a picnic. Bathing in the sea there the parson nearly severed his big toe on an oyster shell. 'I'll do it up for you,' said Sammy. He took a plug of tobacco the parson had been chewing, stuck it in the cut, and tied a handkerchief over it. Sammy told him, 'It'll soon be all right, I think'; and, recalling the incident, added: 'He didn't walk for a week.'

Sammy always fancied himself as a first-aider. During Somerset's victory over Yorkshire in 1903, one of the visitors' bowlers, J.T. Brown jun., put his shoulder out bowling. Sammy related:

I took off my boot and tried to put it [the shoulder] in at once, but couldn't manage it, although I had someone to sit on his head and others to hold him down. He was very sweaty from bowling, I couldn't get a firm grip of his arm, so he had to go to the hospital and have it done. I am certain to this day that had he kept still it would have saved a lot of trouble.

Alas, this ended Brown's cricket career.

Back in England, Braund was a mainstay of the Somerset team, and in 1902 the county won seven matches and climbed to seventh in the table. Sammy was no longer a bowler – his wickets were now costing 30 runs a time and he was taking only ten or so all summer in county games. He was painfully aware of the decline in his bowling over the years. 'A bad fast bowler is the best thing in the world to bat against,' he wrote later, 'and I ought to know. As if maybe I was a good one at one time, I was a bad one for many years. And I can see good batsmen licking their lips when I went on.' There were not so many runs coming, either, although now and then he would produce a sparkling innings.

There was an epic win over Middlesex before a big Whitsun crowd at Lord's. Middlesex made 115, Somerset 123, then Middlesex 320, setting what looked like a hopeless task as Somerset wickets fell. The two Palairets and Braund were out very quickly, and though a recovery followed, Sammy met with roars of laughter on the second night at a dinner given by the Somerset London Society when he said: 'Well, gentlemen, I hope you will come up to Lord's tomorrow and see us win.' As they did, guided by an inspiring innings from Sammy.

When the ninth wicket fell, 16 runs were still needed. The last batsman, Cranfield, was given his orders by his captain as he arrived at the wicket: 'Keep your bat straight and still. Just stop 'em. I'll get the runs.' 'Cranny' was rather overcome by the occasion and was in any case rather excitable. His first ball was outside the off stump, and somehow he directed it to the leg boundary for four. With a few expletives, Sammy made it clear that 'Cranny' would not face another ball. He didn't, and Sammy saw Somerset to victory, his contribution being an undefeated 88.

But sadly it was now becoming clear that his days in first-class cricket were numbered. He said that 1903 was his own worst year at cricket. A knee injury caused by a lady hockey player during a mixed match required an operation, kept him out of several games, and affected his performance in others. He scored just over 200 runs for the county all season at an average of barely more than 10, and took only nine championship wickets. But, still, there were six wins to celebrate, including a further one over Yorkshire.

That summer Sammy made the acquaintance again, this time on home ground, of the Philadelphians. The match was at Bath, and Somerset had a convincing win by 10 wickets, largely due to Braund. For one of the few occasions on the tour, the Americans' famous fast bowler, Barton King, did not come off.

There were more runs for Sammy in 1904, but just four wickets. Two centuries contributed to his total of almost 700 runs. He hit 136 at Taunton off Hampshire, and a fortnight later 123 off the Surrey bowlers. The latter game marked his last appearance at the Oval, where he and Somerset had accomplished so much. He enjoyed some luck in that farewell innings, some of his mishits falling away from fielders; and he had the satisfaction of leading the county to an innings victory. Next month Surrey were beaten by seven wickets at Taunton.

Later that same summer Sammy received news from Australia that his father had died at his home in Manly. John Woods, who was 76, did not specifically mention Sammy in his will, which ran to several pages. But he did not exclude him, as he did Sammy's eldest brother, Harry, whose mode of life John did not approve of. Nevertheless it is possible that Sammy may have received some further financial help as the will, a rather complicated one, gave absolute discretion to the trustees to pay sums to any of the children, barring Harry.

Somerset's improvement in the championship ended the following summer, that of 1905. Sammy had to call on 31 players, and seldom was there a strong enough team in the field. Of 18 championship matches Somerset won just one. Altogether he used 23 bowlers. He bowled himself hardly at all, and took two wickets all season, at a cost of 88.5 runs each. But he did better with the bat, with a century (125 off Sussex at Bath) among his 700 runs.

At the end of the year he announced that he would be giving up the captaincy after the 1906 season.

In his final year of leading the county, Somerset did a little better, but Sammy's own contribution again declined. He did not quite reach 500 runs, and his bowling figures were: 0 wickets, 62 runs. *Wisden* declared that it would not be easy for Somerset to find another leader possessed of 'the same inspiring qualities', and: 'More than anyone else Woods has been the making of Somerset cricket.'

Judged solely by statistics, his captaincy had not been a triumph.

Fewer than a quarter of the county championship matches in those 13 seasons had been won, and for every game won two were lost. Somerset were never out of the bottom half of the table at the end of any season. A couple of times there was no one below them. Yet could anyone else have done better with the resources available? There were times when he seemed to carry the team on his shoulders, and he always led by example. Would anyone else have inspired Somerset to those dramatic wins over Surrey and Yorkshire? And certainly it could never be said that Somerset were slow scorers or a dull side to watch.

Some of his contemporaries rated him highly as a leader. Midway through Sammy's years as captain, Fry, in *Giants of the Game* (1899), called him 'the best captain imaginable' and said that none knew more of the game or used his knowledge better. 'He has boundless enthusiasm and the power of infusing a strong solution of it into others. What is more he tries every ounce and makes others try also.'

Jessop, who played under him in that momentous Gentlemen v. Players match, said: 'A more inspiring leader I could not wish for', and ranked him high as a county captain, always contriving to make the best use of his limited bowling resources.

Jephson, who played with Sammy at Cambridge and later led Surrey, said: 'He was the best captain I ever played under; he was the personification of keenness, the apotheosis of fairness, and his capacity for getting his side out of a cleft stick was proverbial.' Jephson added that there were two individuals Sammy could never stand: the 'funk' and the 'slacker'. He had no time for either.

Peter Roebuck, who captained Somerset 80 summers later, wrote in his book about the county, *From Sammy to Jimmy*: 'Woods sits in history as an alert and imaginative captain', but found him 'a man incapable of building the strength of his team by finding outside talent'. This was indeed his, and for years to come, Somerset's weakness. It was partly due to a reluctance to rely much on professionals; and this in turn was only partly due to the question of money. Not until after the 1914–18 war, under John Daniell, did the county attract more talent. For even longer it lagged behind other counties in the number of professionals employed.

When it was know that Sammy was to give up the captaincy, a fund was launched for his benefit. In the lunch interval of the first match of 1907 at Taunton, against Yorkshire, a cheque was handed to him, together with an illuminated address. Contributions had come from many parts of the country.

The illuminated address, the work of local craftsmen, was thus described in the local newspapers:

> The address is executed in gold and colours and is most appropriately designed, the exquisite border being reminiscent of the monastic work of several centuries ago. The prominent feature of the address is the centre panel at the head, which contains a watercolour drawing of the Somerset County Cricket Ground, surmounted by a shield bearing the badge of the club, the golden dragon of Wessex. The initial letter to the text of the address surrounds a characteristic colour photograph of 'Sammy' in one of his happiest moods, and on either side of the address are introduced into the border two small plaques representing a batsman and a bowler, while at the bottom corners are drawings of the pavilions at the Oval and Lord's cricket grounds. In the centre of the bottom is an escutcheon bearing the monogram of the recipient. The whole . . . is placed in a massive frame of dead English gilt.

The text recalled his long connection with Somerset cricket and 'the sportsmanlike manner in which you have captained the XI'.

The amount raised was £1,620, of which, wisely – since Sammy admitted he was no good with money – £1,250 was invested by trustees for his benefit. The balance was handed over to him. There was a laudatory speech by a local dignitary, Mr C.E.J. Esdaile, a former master of West Somerset Foxhounds, frequently punctuated by (Applause) and (Loud Applause) and (Hear, Hear). Sammy said in reply that anything he had done for Somerset cricket and rugby had been the greatest pleasure to him and he had enjoyed himself from the very first moment he came to the county. 'I am sorry that my bowling went off in the way it did so quickly, but I have tried my best to get a side together, which is a great difficulty in Somerset.'

An enterprising local photographer recorded the presentation, hurried back to his studio, and before the end of the day had on sale postcards which were being posted that very evening.

The £1,620 was not quite as much as the organisers had hoped for, but in comparison with the benefits of the period it was not at all bad. Very few amateurs received a benefit at all. Lord Hawke had a bit more from his, but MacLaren less; and it was a good deal more than a star professional from any but the wealthier counties could expect.

Little as it seems now, £1,620 was a considerable sum in 1907. The local newspapers reporting the occasion carried many advertisements showing that one could rent a good house for a few shillings a week, a cook could be employed for £20 a year, a housemaid for half that; and while a ton of coal cost just over £1, a gallon of Scotch whisky (or 20 gallons of beer if you preferred) was less.

No less appreciated by Sammy was a further presentation during a break in a match against the South Africans at Bath in August. Lionel Palairet, who had taken over as captain that year, handed him a gold watch as a memento of his captaincy. It had been subscribed by all who had played under his leadership. The *County Gazette* reported: 'The matter had been kept a strict secret, so it was a treat to see Woods' face when he was handed the watch.'

In that match against the South Africans, Sammy took a wicket, but from the time he gave up the captaincy until he finally retired altogether from first-class cricket three years later he did not bowl a single over in championship matches. Only occasionally in those years, either, was there a glimpse of his old form as a batsman.

Given the team he inherited, it was not surprising that Palairet had no more success as captain. After one season he was to hand over to Daniell, a hard-hitting batsman who was also an outstanding rugby man and, like Sammy, captained the England XV. But he, too, over the next few years could do no better, though certainly he could not be faulted for his efforts as either leader or player.

Although Sammy was no longer captain, there was an unusual match in that summer of 1907 in which his influence can be sensed. It was against the old foe, Gloucester, captained by Gilbert Jessop. Rain prevented play on the first day, only an hour was possible on the second, and then the start was delayed for an hour on the third. Forcing the pace, Gloucester scored 139 and declared with five wickets down, then dismissed Somerset for 72, with Sammy top scoring with 18. Gloucester quickly hit 47 for 4 and declared again, leaving Somerset to get 115 in an hour and a quarter.

They could have sat tight and made a comfortable draw, but for years it had been Sammy's dictum that draws were no good. They went for the runs, losing wickets quickly. Sammy was again top scorer, hitting 29 before being caught off Jessop. Unfortunately, though, towards the end the spirit of the game changed, and although victory was not impossible, Somerset cautiously played out time, finishing on 102 for 8. Had Sammy still been captain, one fancies the remaining

116

batsmen would have had positive orders to continue to go for the runs.

Jessop's bold tactics, unheard of in those days, nearly paid off, and Sammy can be pictured commiserating with him afterwards. In later years such declarations ceased to be regarded as 'curious cricket', as one writer called it.

There was one other memorable match that season. It involved Sammy's fellow Australian, Albert Trott, who, like Sammy, had played for both Australia and England. It was his benefit match at Lord's, and Middlesex's opponents were Somerset.

A remarkable spell of bowling by Trott gave Middlesex victory. In the second innings he took four wickets in four balls (Sammy was the third victim, being deceived in the flight and bowled). His next ball clipped a stump but failed to remove a bail. Trott had not finished: within half an hour he had performed a second hat-trick. After the match Sammy gave him a straw hat. Hand painted on the band were seven rabbits bolting into the pavilion. Trott treasured it and wore the hat in games that season.

Sammy's first-class swan song really came the following summer, even though he still played a few matches more. But the season had hardly begun before he received news of the death, at the age of 55, of his former 'guardian', Gilbert Burrington, the cricket-loving banker who had influenced the direction of Sammy's life. At the funeral in Bridgwater, attended by many of the leading citizens, Sammy – himself one of the town's best-known personalities – was with the family mourners. One of Gilbert's sons in particular, Humphrey, was a close friend for many years. He, too, was a keen cricketer and, at Sammy's invitation, had played five games for Somerset early in the century, although without distinction.

In the summer of 1908, Somerset recorded two wins in 20 matches and finished bottom, but the match at Southampton in August, and Sammy's part in it, was one to remember. Hampshire had made 425, and after dismissing Somerset for 262 made the mistake of not enforcing the follow on. A slow-medium bowler, William Greswell, so troubled the Hampshire batsmen in the second innings with his late swing from the off that they were all out for 128 (Greswell 7 for 42). Needing 292 to win, Somerset were soon in trouble themselves, losing three wickets cheaply.

Sammy, who had batted at No. 8 in the first innings, now came in to join Braund. In two and a half hours they put on 199 to win the day by seven wickets. Sammy contributed 105 and Braund took his total to 124. Both gave chances as they hit out. Sammy recalled that they ran 'short runs' – 'what I call bustled 'em up. Some shocking runs we ran . . . and my poor old legs did give me trouble that night. But we had quite a lot of overthrows.' Both were credited with a dozen fours.

Sammy was now turned 40 and all that running left him with cramp as he travelled by train to Exeter that night. 'I had cramp all the way, and if it hadn't been for meeting a farmer pal who had some whisky and rubbed the calves of my legs I think I would have fainted,' he said. 'This finished me for the season.'

But for his physical tribulations, Sammy might have played as a batsman for a few more seasons (after all, Grace played first-class cricket through his fifties). It was sometimes a struggle in his last few years. When asked how he was, he would reply: 'My side's a bit strained, my left knee's got water on it, and I've got rheumatism in my neck, still I'm pretty fit, me dear, thank you.'

In his previous 13 innings that summer, before the century at Southampton, Sammy had made only about 150 runs. The next season, 1909, he made a single appearance, batting at No. 8 and scoring one run in a drawn match with Yorkshire at Bath. He also took a catch. That was his final county game before his home supporters.

The end came in 1910, a terrible year for Somerset in which they failed to win a match. Sammy played three times, early in the season, each match ending in heavy defeat. The first two were in Sheffield and Manchester, and his last game was at Lord's. Against Yorkshire he opened the batting and scored 16 and 10, being run out in the second innings. His last appearance of all came on June 13 and 14 against Middlesex. He scored a duck in the first innings, 10 in the second.

It was a sad ending to his long career. The spirit was ever willing; the flesh was not. He finished one short of 300 matches for Somerset in the county's first-class years, which had started way back in 1891.

With the bat he scored 12,637 runs in 522 innings for Somerset (18 not out), and his average was 25.07. His 19 first-class centuries were all for the county, if one stretches a point and considers his first, in 1891, for 'Hewett's Team' at Cambridge as being for a Somerset side. In all his 401 first-class matches (1886–1910) he had 690 innings (35 not out) and scored 15,352 runs at 23.43.

His bowling record for Somerset was 554 wickets at an average of 23.78 (and he also took another 137 wickets for the county in its pre-first-class years); and in all first-class appearances 1,040 wickets at 20.82. For Somerset he took five or more wickets in an innings 36 times, and he did the same on a further 40 occasions in other first-class fixtures. He took 205 catches for Somerset, and 282 altogether.

There could have been few other regular county players of his day who played at the same time in so many other matches – for teams ranging from the Free Foresters to village clubs – and with such enthusiasm. Jessop said that Sammy rarely declined to play 'in any other old match' that came along. 'No day was ever too long for Sam, nor was he entirely happy unless in the open air,' he said.

Back in September 1901 Sammy and Jessop appeared in a benefit match at Bedminster, Bristol, the teams being made up mainly of Somerset and Gloucester players. The two hit 142 runs in 22 minutes before Jessop, slightly ahead in runs, was stumped.

On another visit to Bristol Sammy got told off for smoking. The incident was related by Essex and Gloucester player Dick Keigwin, who was for many years a master at the city's Clifton College. Sammy went there to play against a college team. In the lunch interval he produced a pipe, unaware that smoking was not allowed anywhere in the college grounds. The headmaster swiftly asked him to put it out. Sammy replied ('in plaintive terms – always a schoolboy in spirit' said Keigwin): 'Well, sir, this is the first time since I was eight that I have been stopped smoking.'

One trait in Sammy's character which surprised those who knew only his usual carefree attitude was his insistence on punctuality, even in these lesser games. If Bridgwater was playing away and the horse brake was to leave with the team at noon, it would leave at noon, even with some of the team missing. They would have to get there by cycle or however else they could.

Sammy ran what he called his Farmers' XI to play in various towns throughout the Westcountry. He had the help of two or three of the Somerset professionals, and the rest of the team would be farmers. They usually won, and would finish the day with dinner and a sing-song.

One of Sammy's stories, one in which (as was often the case) the facts have doubtless been improved upon, tells how he had three big farmers – all about 6ft 3in, he said – in the team, and:

> Just before the game started three white ducks crossed the wicket. I remarked to them it was a bad omen. They didn't understand until, I having put them in 1, 2, and 3, they all

got bowled first ball. I had the ducks killed and placed one in each of their bags.

As well as the Farmers' XI he sometimes played with the Moon-lighters, a touring team captained by the former Somerset pro-fessional, Nichols. And there were still the country-house matches to enjoy.

One anecdote, the truth of which cannot be disputed, concerns the second time in his career he took all 10 wickets in an innings. (He also took 10 wickets in New York, but there were then 16 in the home team). He was playing for a team at Halswell Park, in the Quantocks, the seat of Lord Wharton:

> Our side got about 90. Lunch was then taken. Our captain put me on first. Whether it was the '76 port our opponents had imbibed of too freely or not I know not. They hadn't played against lobs before, and one after the other tried to hit me for eight or ten each ball. I took all 10 wickets for a very few runs. The match appeared in the *Sportsman* two days afterwards with a comment from the cricket corre-spondent, congratulating me, and very pleased to know that I had regained my lost form of the last few years.

Sammy continued to play cricket whenever he could in the remaining years, rheumatism permitting, and tennis, too. Perhaps his last match of any consequence was just before the 1914–18 war when he appeared for one of the Westcountry's oldest clubs, Lansdown, at Bath. The visitors were the M.C.C., and Sammy's second innings knock of 60 just failed to save the day.

Neville Cardus, recalling that great win by Sammy's men over Yorkshire in 1901, was to write: 'Is it not sinful that such a man as Woods, with his love of cricket and the sun, should ever be taken out of the light into the shadow of age.'

Sammy at War

It was after that exciting win over Hampshire in 1908, in which he scored his last century, that Sammy 'learnt of the war to come'. He had been invited aboard a yacht at Weymouth, and following the match travelled there by train via Exeter.

After lunch in a Weymouth hotel, Sammy met some German officers from a gunboat which was lying offshore. He recalled:

> One of them asked me to have a drink. I did, a whisky and soda, they were drinking crême de menthe. After a few the senior officer, one with a beard, drank to 'The Day'. I asked him which day. 'The day we fight England on the sea,' he said. I told him we were their best customers. He said, 'Maybe, but it must come. There is one thing the English cannot do,' he said, 'drink', so naturally we had some more. Well, to cut a long story short, about four-thirty it took the landlord, the boots, a policeman and myself to get these gentlemen into their boat safely. I often laughed about it afterwards and wondered if he thought there was one fellow in England who could, as he said, 'do thee gargle'.

On the day that war came six years later, on August 4 1914, Somerset, struggling around the bottom of the championship table, lost to their old rivals Gloucester at Bristol. Not for the first or last time, Somerset were in trouble off the field, too, and to try to improve their financial position had launched a shilling fund which brought in a very valuable £500. They were also busy as war started, making final arrangements for their first cricket week at Weston-super-Mare.

The declaration of war as the German army marched into Belgium and the Old Contemptibles hurried off to fight came when the counties each had several fixtures to play. Surrey and Middlesex were competing for top place. Nearly all the fixtures were completed, though Surrey had to finish their home games at Lord's as the military

121

took over the Oval. One of Somerset's matches was cancelled, but the Weston festival week went ahead.

With war overshadowing everything (reports of county matches in *The Times* were often reduced to three or four lines) and the first casualty lists being published, there were many who felt that cricket should declare its innings closed. But the secretary of the M.C.C. in a statement two days after war started had said that 'no good purpose can be served at the present moment by cancelling matches unless the services of those engaged in cricket who have no military training can be utilized in their country's service.'

Within a week of war starting Lord Kitchener, with the slogan 'Your King and Country Need you', called for 100,000 to join the colours. And as the first of the Old Contemptibles were dying across the sea, W.G. Grace spoke out in *The Sportsman*. Sammy would have read:

> The fighting on the Continent is very severe and is likely to be prolonged. I think the time has arrived when the county cricket season should be closed, for it is not fitting at a time like this that able-bodied men should be playing day by day, and pleasure-seekers look on. There are so many who are young and able, and are still hanging back. I should like to see all first-class cricketers of suitable age set a good example, and come to the help of their country without delay in its hour of need.

The season did not close immediately as Grace wished, but many cricketers were soon off to war and their names were beginning to appear in the roll of honour in the newspapers. Before Christmas three young men who had played for Somerset were already dead in France and Belgium. One was Lieut. Ralph Escott Hancock, aged 26, killed in action at Festubert in October, one of the Hancock family of Wiveliscombe to which Sammy was so attached.

It was not only the younger ones who were soon in uniform. Jessop at once volunteered and was commissioned in the 14th Manchester Regiment. One of the last photographs of Grace taken in 1915 shows him with MacLaren and Ranji, both in Army uniform. That summer Captain Jessop and Lieut. MacLaren took part in a successful recruiting campaign.

Sammy hardly needed any exhortation from Grace or anyone else. His difficulty was in getting the Army to have him. He was now in his

48th year, a few years older and rather less fit than Jessop and MacLaren. Within a few weeks he had tried to enlist in several places in Wales and the Midlands. 'But I was always spotted, and failed to pass the age test,' he said.

However, Sammy was fortunate in having friends in military places, and in November 'a pal at headquarters' got him a commission in the Somerset Light Infantry, whose depot was in Taunton. He was somehow pronounced fit 'except for slight varicose veins'; and he kept quiet about his rheumatism and other afflictions. For the next four years he was in uniform, latterly as a captain in the Labour Corps, forerunner of the Royal Pioneer Corps.

Cardus's picture of Sammy loading cannon in the Dardanelles while men lay dying around him is what might have been, not what was; a bit of Cardus licence. As Peter Roebuck puts it in his history of Somerset cricket, 'the image fits the man'. Despite his age, and although he saw no action, Sammy had a fairly active time. No doubt he was the life and soul of many a mess, and this giant of the cricket and rugby fields was regarded with respect, even awe, by the men who served with him. He engaged in sport when he had the opportunity, and played a fair amount of cricket.

Sammy wrote, a few years later, under the heading 'Soldiering', a short and tantalisingly sketchy account of his experiences. His first unit was the 6th Somersets, one of the new battalions hastily raised in response to Kitchener's call. It was commanded by Lt. Col. C.G. Rawling, who when war started had been in command of the regimental depot at Taunton and who perhaps had something to do with Sammy's arrival in uniform. Rawling later commanded a brigade and was killed in France in 1917.

The 6th Somersets did most of their training that first autumn and winter of war at Aldershot. Sammy had 'a sorry time' for a while in the slush and mud, even though, he said, he had done plenty of wild-fowl shooting when he had often been 'up to my middle'. Of those early Army days he wrote:

> What a place it was! Living in wooden huts (how quickly they got them up), a quagmire between each hut, all the men in blue except the officers, not a few of whom were, like myself, new to the game, and I may say we studied it just as much as we had ever studied games of all sorts, and there was just as much luck, or even more so, than in any game I have ever played. I was taken in hand by the

sergeant-major, and put through my paces. Duck-boards there were all over the place. If one fell off a board it meant a bath. The German air raids soon came along, and lights were out soon after five o'clock. We played bridge in the evenings after mess, and of course sometimes before. The rule was that no rubber should be started after nine o'clock.

Shortly before ten one evening, after playing bridge from four o'clock, Sammy was returning to his hut when he fell into a drain which had not been there earlier. He lay there unconscious a long time and woke up with a bad cut on his head. He called for help and was found by a guard.

In a night exercise the company Sammy was with had to make an attack, in field kit, on a waterworks. After crawling about for an hour, they 'up and charged'. The company would have been in trouble had it been the real thing, for Sammy, tired of crouching down, had got up and shown his figure to the defenders too soon and given things away. 'I wonder how many of our poor fellows died during the war through doing exactly as I had done to our friendly enemies,' he said.

Indeed it would seem unlikely that Sammy would have survived long had he been a younger man and seen front-line action. His bravery on the sports field was legendary, and he had a streak of impetuosity. When young officers serving with him said, 'Hell, I am sick of this, when are we going to France?' he told them not to fret but wait to go to Berlin with 'Mr. 'Oods and party'. Well, Mr Woods never got to France, except to take drafts to Etaples. 'If he had done so you wouldn't most likely be reading this,' he wrote years later.

Sammy was no lover of military red tape, or any other sort either; a man of his nature could hardly be expected to be. A friend who saw him off when he left to take his first draft to France met him on the return. After a long and tedious journey he had safely delivered the men. They were at once required to do something that necessitated their waiting around indefinitely. Sammy was 'furious' and went to the brasshats to tell them this was all nonsense. 'Why, the men have had nothing to eat or drink since – ' he told them. He had a few things to say, and rather fell into disfavour. Where he was known, allowances would be made for his reaction to what seemed to him some silly piece of officialdom. But if his superiors did not appreciate that they were dealing with Sammy Woods, difficulties could arise.

The 6th battalion moved to France in May 1915 and was soon in action, but before then Sammy had been transferred to the 9th battalion at St Austell, in Cornwall, which later became the 45th Territorial Reserve Battalion and ceased to wear the Somersets' badge. He was subsequently quartered at Wareham, in Dorset, where 'we made a capital cricket pitch'.

Sammy remembered his days at St. Austell:

> A splendid little place, had there not been so many tee-totallers and Methody people in it. However, lots of them were good sports and hospitable . . . We had most comfortable quarters and quite a happy, if strenuous, time at drilling, physical jerks, etc. All the men were taught to swim. Boxing we had galore, and we won the championship of the Southern Command. Funnily enough, six of our ten competitors came from Bridgwater.

From the Somersets Sammy was posted to the 1st Royal Garrison Battalion, Warwickshire, and later sailed from Plymouth en route for Khartoum, spending a year there. 'A more uninteresting spot I never struck,' he said, and was doubtless not unhappy to leave his fellow soldiers behind when he was sent home after suffering malaria.

Sammy never mentioned anything about the Dardanelles, where Cardus had placed him. However, *The Times*, in its obituary of Sammy, recorded:

> On one occasion when he was in a transport at the Dardanelles the weather was so hot that even the Hindu stokers were overcome. Woods called for volunteers, and with seven men descended into the stokehold. He trimmed the coal like an expert for six hours, and outlasted all the rest. This was characteristic of his courage; when in Australia he had saved two lives from shark-infested waters.

E.H.D. Sewell left a brief reference in one of his cricket books to Sammy 'stoking a troopship down the Mediterranean to Alexandria', without mentioning the Dardanelles.

A member of the family in Australia has been unable to find any account of Sammy saving anyone in shark-infested waters; but there is a family tradition – recorded in an Australian newspaper – that on another occasion Sammy saved a boy from drowning in the English Channel, in icy cold conditions which affected Sammy's health.

These incidents were not mentioned in his reminiscences by Sammy himself. In later years, though, he blamed rheumatism which had developed in a hip on a fall he had from a camel in Egypt. 'I was in charge of a bunch of those sods when they stampeded and made for a cactus forest,' he told a friend. 'So off I rolled, and fell a bit wrong.'

While he was in Khartoum one of the jobs that fell to Sammy was that of censor. One cannot imagine him enjoying any desk job. Sewell wrote to him there, seeking a brief reply to some cricket query. It came as follows: 'Dear Sewell. Yes. – dry here. How's things? Cheers. Yrs, Sam.' The punctuation has been added: there was none at all on the half-sheet of paper. Someone else recorded that Sammy had 'very bad writing'.

Sammy had two months leave and went on a shooting trip about 1,000 miles up the Nile. The bag this party claimed included leopards and two lions. He recalled:

> My collection would have been better had I been a better rifle shot. However I was a bit old for the game – 49. We couldn't get any beasts to carry us, and it was frightfully hot, and flies were a bit of a nuisance. Our guides, 'Dinkers', one 6ft 7in, another 6ft 6in, were wonderful fellows. One carried me one day when I was ill, certainly two miles on his back without a halt, and wasn't a bit distressed. The only things against them as shikaris [hunters] is that every time we shot a deer they ate so cheerfully at night and got some strong drink of some kind from goodness only know where, that next morning they were so heavy and sleepy as to be useless and dangerous, as well I know to my cost. I gave one a rifle to carry whilst I was stalking guinea-fowl one day. He got fiddling about with the rifle and sent a bullet between my arm and side. I always made them walk in front of me after that.

There was another incident involving a shikari:

> One day one of the beauties wouldn't obey the cook and collect wood to make a fire to dry our blankets with. Said he: 'Guide, no fireman.' I had him before me after a palaver with the cook. He took up his spear in a very nasty way, pointing in my direction, as I had a revolver handy. I gave him two shillings and sent him home. He lived a hundred and fifty miles away. I hope he got there safely.

Back in England after his malaria, Sammy was attached to the 20th Devons, and was soon looking after the guards at Plymouth. For a time they guarded ammunition works, after which he became a captain in the Labour Corps, at first on Salisbury Plain. He finished the war at Devizes, where again 'we made a capital wicket, and had many good matches'.

Once, when one of Sammy's team was out, he called, 'Who is in next?' 'I am,' said a Tommy. He had not put his pads on yet and was about to. Sammy told him, 'You may go in last, by which time I hope you will be ready.' In the next match, when Sammy, who had opened with the Colonel, was out, he said: 'Next man in.' One got up and proceeded to the wicket. Sammy looked – and saw there were four more all waiting with their pads already on.

Many of the young men with whom Sammy had trained and spent the early months of 1915, waiting for overseas postings, never returned. The war claimed, too, the lives of many of the cricketers he had played with, including Leonard Moon, the Middlesex player who Sammy had chased with a knife round a house in Hampstead in one of his pranks.

A dozen or so Somerset cricketers had died in the war. Among them was a struggling professional, Frederick Percey Hardy, who in 1916 took his own life while on leave in London, unable to face returning to the horrors of war in the trenches.

And as well as those who died as a result of the war, there were other old friends of the cricket world he was to see no more, foremost among them Grace and Stoddart who, sadly, with health and money worries, had shot himself. His Cambridge room-mate, Gregor MacGregor, did not long survive the war, dying in 1919 a few days before his 50th birthday.

Beyond the Boundary

T he war over, Sammy was foremost among a handful of men dedicated to cricket who took responsibility for getting Somerset back on the field in the spring of 1919. And the very first game at Taunton in that first year of peace provided perhaps the most bizarre ending to a match in the history of the county championship; a dramatic, controversial finish which might not have occurred but for Sammy.

The match, between Somerset and Sussex in May, ended in a tie, a rare enough happening in county games. But the excitement over the result was overshadowed by the confusion surrounding the fate of the last batsman, who was dismissed from the game in a manner never before known in first-class cricket in England, and never since repeated.

The match had been one of fluctuating fortunes, right up to that controversial last minute, or, to be more precise, four minutes. The home county was led on this occasion by 'Farmer' Jack White, later to captain England. His team included Braund, one of four professionals. Sussex also had four professionals, among them a young off-break bowler and more than useful batsman, Maurice Tate, who was to make his reputation later when he developed into a fast-medium bowler. On this occasion he starred with the bat: his 69 was the highest score in the match and helped to set the scene for the climax.

It was one of the Sussex amateurs, who scored no runs, took no wickets, and held no catches, who provided the headlines. He was Harold Heygate, aged 34, who had previously played for the county a few times in his late teens and early twenties. Serving in the war he suffered a leg wound and this and rheumatism which developed were to end his career. The Taunton match was his sixth and last in first-class cricket. He may even have been brought into the team just to make up the number.

As an experiment, county matches in 1919 were of two days only. Batting first, on May 21, a Wednesday, Somerset scored 243; then dismissed the visitors for 242. In their second innings Somerset collapsed: 103 all out.

Sussex, needing 105 to win, were soon struggling too, and at one stage on the Thursday afternoon were 48 for 6. The captain, Herbert Wilson, who had opened, was going well, and a partnership with a professional, Harry Roberts, took the score to 103 before the latter went. No. 9 was out without scoring, and amid intense excitement a run was scrambled and the scores were level. Then White deceived the new batsman, and nine wickets were down.

Only Heygate had not batted. In Somerset's first innings he fielded with a bad limp, and when Sussex went in he came in last and was bowled without scoring. A substitute fielded for him throughout Somerset's second innings, and it was generally understood that he would take no further part in the game. An M.C.C. inquiry into what happened showed that the umpires had been told that only 10 would bat in Sussex's second innings.

Consequently, when No. 10 was dismissed, one of the umpires, Alfred Street, a former Surrey professional, removed the bails and the players turned to walk off.

Suddenly they were halted by a sign from the pavilion. What was happening? The crowd, who had started to leave their seats, paused and many sat down again. They could not see the activity in the pavilion, at which Sammy was at the centre.

Then, from the pavilion, still clad in the blue serge trousers of his suit, a waistcoat with watch and chain, and wearing a tie, there slowly limped the figure of Harold Heygate.

After what seemed an age, and was in fact probably as many as four minutes from the fall of the last wicket, he reached the crease. (Strangely, accounts do not mention him being accompanied by a runner.)

White returned to the end from which he was bowling . . . but then came new consternation among the crowd. Before Heygate could take guard, umpire Street again removed the bails and pulled up the stumps. The match was over; Heygate was recorded as 'absent'; and the result was not a draw but a tie.

The next day the 'sensation' was reported in all the newspapers, which explained that although both captains had been willing to carry on playing, Street had ruled that Heygate had exceeded the two minutes permitted to reach the wicket. (Today his dismissal from the game would be recorded as 'timed out'). It subsequently emerged that Street made this decision in response to an appeal by a Somerset player, still later identified as Braund, who had called out: 'How about the time? He's taken over two minutes.'

The reports were mingled with comment and criticism (including, inevitably, 'it's not cricket') and the issue became an emotive one. *Wisden* called it 'an extraordinary and in some respects very regrettable incident.'

Sammy did not think much of it, either. Watching from the pavilion, he had called out 'Shame!' when Street and the other umpire, Fred Roberts, an old Gloucester player, ended the game. He had reason not to think much of their decision, for, as Tate related in his reminiscences, Sammy ('always a great sportsman') had urged Heygate to go out and try to get the winning run (or at least keep his end up while his captain did so). But more than that, it seems, Sammy helped Heygate to put on his pads. Perhaps there had stirred in Sammy's memory that moment 20 years earlier when he was captaining the Gentlemen and had bowled that extra over after 6.30 on the final day to make sure someone won the match, even if were the Players.

Although no formal appeal was made to the M.C.C., its committee decided in 'the public interest' to find the facts. Its eventual statement concluded by saying it upheld the umpires' decision.

Sammy recorded an amusing sequel at Bristol in the very next match. The same umpires were standing, and, Sammy wrote, in several instances a new batsman met the departing batsman 20 yards from the pavilion – an eagerness to get to the wicket of which he approved.

There was a further very strange occurrence back at Taunton a match or two later that season when Gloucester arrived to play Somerset. Inevitably Sammy would have known what was going on, even if he were not, as was very likely, more closely involved.

One of the Somerset players had stood down at a late stage, and his place was taken by someone called S. Trimnell. He contributed handsomely to his team's victory, scoring 92 and 58 not out. No one had heard of Trimnell before, yet he was more than familiar to many spectators. He was, in fact, Sydney Rippon, one of twins who were solid opening batsmen for the county. The reason he assumed another name (in fact that of his grandmother) was that at the time he was on sick leave from the Civil Service. It was not thought right his name should appear on the Somerset scoresheet if he were not fit for work. The ruse, inevitably, was soon known and caused a great deal of amusement. Fortunately the Civil Service was forgiving. 'Trimnell' was replaced by 'Rippon' in accounts of the match, and all was well.

At the end of that year, 1919, Sammy was appointed secretary of the club, a role for which, as Roebuck observes in his history of the county, he was 'wholly unsuited'. It was an appointment made more because of his reputation than his administrative ability. Certainly, however, he helped to put the club back into operation after the war. One of his first acts was to launch a £500 appeal to pay for restoring the ground after the ravages of war. It had been used by troops, including his fellow Australians, and a lot of repairs needed doing. There had been much damage to seats and the pavilion and stands.

Vic Robson, then a boy and son of the long-time Somerset professional Ernie Robson, recalls Sammy calling at their house in Taunton to discuss getting cricket going again. One problem also was that the ground had become infested with rabbits, and Vic remembers his father going there with a gun and dog to deal with them. One fancies that Sammy, who liked shooting, joined in.

The ground staff found Sammy an exacting taskmaster. One of its young members recalled long afterwards that when work on preparing for a match was behind the clock (the work, actually, was getting ready tennis courts and a croquet lawn for members attending the game), he was summoned to the secretary's presence. Sammy roared at him: 'If you don't get everything straightened out by tomorrow, you've got the sack.'

Sammy was doubtless good at getting things done like this. The heavy roller was usually pulled by a horse, but if the animal was not available he would send down to the Labour Exchange for some men to do it. Sammy also had considerable persuasive powers in getting someone to do this or that for him. But when it came to finance and committees and paper work, he was hardly the right man for the job.

When a friend asked him why he could not get a particular thing done, Sammy replied: 'Me? What's the use? Whenever I make a suggestion on committee some deaf old so-and-so who was in charge in Delhi ups and downs it.'

Probably Sammy's own financial situation had a a bearing on his decision to take the secretaryship. His only other income now he was a civilian again would seem to have been something from the money invested by the trustees of his benefit fund, unless there was help as well from the trustees of his father's estate. In his will there was a reference to some Japanese bonds acquired at some time. In his first year as secretary of Somerset county cricket club, the accounts show that Sammy received as salary and expenses £246. This was about 10 per cent of the club's expenditure. The salaries of the professionals totalled £460 and the wages of the county ground staff just over £200.

On the field Somerset were having better times now, much of the improvement being due to the leadership of Daniell and his recruitment of talented amateurs, both local and from the universities. But the finances were a headache, and it was perhaps a relief and not even a surprise to members of the county committee when, at the annual meeting early in 1923, Sammy 'sprung upon the meeting' (according to the Press) his resignation.

When he had been appointed, he said, there had been many doubts as to his business capabilities, and he felt those doubts had proved well founded. The president, Arthur Newton, who had often stood behind the stumps to Sammy's deliveries, said the club owed him a great debt for all he had done for Somerset. But he added that county cricket management nowadays needed business training, and in the circumstances there was no other course than to accept his resignation. Efforts were made to persuade Sammy to serve on the committee, but in the end he did not. In an editorial, the *Somerset County Gazette* summed things up: 'As Mr. Woods candidly recognised, there is an element of business in sport, and he modestly confesses that a man stronger in business qualities might serve the club better.'

If he did not like the committees and the paper work and the business responsibilities, one part of his job Sammy really did enjoy was in taking County and Ground teams around Somerset. In his last summer as secretary he took them to 11 venues. He himself did not play so much cricket now, although occasionally he turned out in local club and village matches.

Sammy liked his 'country cricket', as he called it, even though his aches and pains restricted his mobility. He bowled almost only lobs nowadays, but got wickets with them. Writing in his late 50s, he said: 'Only last season I got six out in an innings, and I can't go out of a walk owing to a bad hip.'

Often now he found himself taking part in a match as umpire, a job he regarded as 'not a happy one', nor an easy one. He added, though: 'I am getting quite good at the business, but am afraid I cheat equally well for both sides through giving advice to bowlers which I didn't ought to.'

One story of Sammy's umpiring was told by Jack MacBryan, a talented Somerset batsmen through the 1920s. It was a country house match at Orchard Portman, near Taunton, in which MacBryan opened the batting against Lord Portman's side. He played in his usual correct style, and was surprised after a while to be told by the umpire: 'It's time you were out, Jack. Hit up a catch to Eddie (Portman)'. Though surprised by this instruction from Sammy, MacBryan did as he was told. Unfortunately the aristocratic fielder dropped the catch. Sammy looked at the batsman. 'He should have held it. So you're out!' he said. A bewildered MacBryan returned to the pavilion. When asked how he was out, he thought for a second or two and said: 'Because Sam said so.' There it was!

Himself a rich character, MacBryan started his first-class career as Sammy's ended, and he acknowledged the great help Sammy gave him in his cricket. In one match at Taunton against Sussex, MacBryan was in all sorts of trouble against the bowling of Maurice Tate. He survived several chances, and coming in to lunch was greeted by Sammy with: 'What the hell do you think you're doing out there?' MacBryan replied that he didn't know which way the ball was going. Sammy called for several balls, took MacBryan to the nets, and spent the rest of the lunch interval bowling underarm at him, moving the ball to leg and off, and all the time giving him advice. MacBryan missed his lunch, but was 'eternally grateful' to Sammy.

Indeed MacBryan regarded Sammy as a great influence on his cricket, and there was mutual affection. When the two met in a club in London one day and MacBryan said he was going to give up county cricket, Sammy wept.

Orchard Portman, a few miles from Taunton, where MacBryan was the victim of that unusual umpiring decision, was well known to Sammy. He had a very good friend, and the source of many invitations, in 'Eddie' – the Right Hon. Edward Claud Berkeley Portman, who succeeded to the viscountcy on his father's death in 1929.

Portman 'looked after him well' is the belief of Vic Robson. Did just a tiny part of the Portman revenues (there were vast estates in Somerset and adjoining counties and property in London's West End) sometimes come Sammy's way?

Eddie Portman, apart from a great love of horses and hunting, liked his cricket, and occasionally played for the Somerset Stragglers. This amateur club, still going strong, was formed in 1900 with Sammy among its founder members. The names of other leading Somerset players can be found here and there in its scorebooks.

Portman enjoyed village cricket, too, and it was doubtless due to his association with the little club at Broadway, in South Somerset, that a now portly Sammy, well into his 50s, is seen in a fading newspaper photograph walking out to bat there, a happy smile on his face. After Sammy's death his aristocratic friend raised a team of well-known players through the 1930s to play in an annual match at Broadway in his memory.

Most of Sammy's cricket now, and his other sport, too, excepting for some golf and bowls, was as a spectator. There was, apart from cricket, always rugby, and he enjoyed the races and attending boxing tournaments. Soccer he became less interested in – there was too much passing now, not enough dribbling, he felt. He stopped paying his ten shillings to be vice-president of a local soccer club when he found that the players were taken to the ground, a mere half a mile, in a charabanc, which waited for them and took them back; at a cost to the club of 15s.

As a spectator he was by no means a silent one. He liked to let his views be known, usually verbally to those around him, and sometimes in interviews. He had even sent a short letter to *The Times* back in 1921 during the Test series in which Australia won three and drew two against an England side which over the series saw 30 players selected. He defended the Test selectors (who included Daniell), who, he said, had a difficult task 'not made any easier by people writing to the papers and giving their ideas of the team that should be picked, and also writing as to how to play fast bowling and how not to.' If there was less rubbish written, he was sure England would do much better.

C.H.B. Pridham, who sometimes played for the Stragglers despite the handicap of a severe war wound, recalled in his book *The Charm of Cricket* that Sammy was always to be seen at Somerset's home matches. He was 'easily the most noticeable spectator wherever he sat, with his familiar figure, his grey head ever hatless, and his deep voice.' He would sometimes be with his close friends and cricket acquaintances; at other times he would join the ordinary folk in the sixpenny seats. Often his voice would ring out across the ground with an encouraging 'We-ell hit!' He would be severe on a delinquent who walked across the screen or behind the bowler's arm. 'Sit down – there!' was a fierce command instantly obeyed.

Another frequenter of the Taunton ground remembered Sammy sitting high in the main stand making those around him laugh with his sporting and country-house stories which he told in a loud monopolistic voice. Sammy was not one who lacked attention (or wanted to).

Oddly, memories of that voice differ among the few who still recall him. One says the Sydney twang was still evident; another that it had gone without trace. Certainly he had acquired the Somerset turn of phrase, however. Vic Robson remembers a 'deep, rugged voice', and no one disagrees that it was a strong and commanding voice which could be heard across a cricket ground.

In these later years Sammy was living in Taunton, with a room or so in a pub or hotel, notably the George (now no longer) in the High Street, whose proprietors were friends. It is said that he often drank a bottle of whisky a day now, partly at least to alleviate his pains. He went daily to the County Club, on a town centre site now occupied by a multiple store. Its members included professional and business men as well as those who did not need to work. Here there were billiards and a bar for a 'gargle' and an exchange of stories, punctuated by his unquenchable laughter. One of Sammy's godsons, Nigel Daniell, thinks he may in fact at one time have lived there. In reference books his address for mail was sometimes given as the County Club. This was not really necessary, for a letter addressed to just 'Mr. Sam, Somerset' would be delivered without any problem by the postmen.

Not being a great letter writer, Sammy probably had little contact with his four or five surviving brothers and sisters in Australia. His mother, the Irish blacksmith's daughter, had died a year before the war, aged almost 80; and Harris, the younger brother who came to England with him and played for Somerset before it became a first-class county, died in 1917. His closest relationship now was with an older sister, Florence, widow of a building contractor named Dean. She was also nearest in distance, for she lived for many years at Exmouth, within 40 miles of Taunton.

A touching sight in these later years was to see Sammy encounter one of the old professionals with whom he had battled on the cricket field a couple of decades or more earlier. He himself recalled visiting Abel in his shop near the Oval after not seeing him for many years. The conversation went like this:

'Hullo, Bobby, how are you?'

'Well, if it isn't Mr. Sam, and the times you have nearly knocked my head off is wonderful, isn't it?'

'Yes, my dear, and the times you have made my shoulder ache is wonderful too.'

Sammy was never one to stay at home all the time, wherever 'home' might be. There were plenty of invitations and he was a welcome guest in many another's house. One such place was the rather grand establishment kept by 'The Bishop', as he called the Rev. Archdale Palmer Wickham, who kept wicket for Somerset for many years. Almost as colourful a character as Sammy (though a teetotaller), 'The Bishop' became president of the Somerset club and was not above asking a fielder to move if he obscured his view of the game.

Sammy, as we know, loved to sing, and during one of his sojourns with Wickham, they sang Gilbert and Sullivan airs, with a falsetto added by Robertson-Glasgow (a distant relative of the clergyman). Afterwards they would retire to play billiards well into the night. Wickham, Sammy remembered, was ready to play anyone 1,000 up at billiards after keeping wicket all day long, and would generally win, too. 'I shall never forget singing at a concert for him, at Brent Knoll,' he said. 'We had supper and then played 2,000 up, and he beat me by 76. We finished at four o'clock in the morning, and I caught the seven o'clock train to a covert shoot. I never shot better in my life.'

There were visits to other country homes and there were grand dinners to attend, but Sammy was equally happy at harvest homes and village concerts and skittles evenings. The extent of his slightly boisterous conviviality would vary according to the company.

Robertson-Glasgow, a talented all-rounder himself who played, like Sammy (but a generation later), for Cambridge, Somerset, and the Gentlemen, became better known as a cricket correspondent and author of several books. He came to know Sammy well throughout the 1920s, and in his autobiography recalled walking around Taunton with 'Somerset's godfather' on a summer morning before a match. Sammy was, he wrote,

> a lover of life and of nearly all things living. On those walks, he would take you into the back parlours of little shops and inquire after the youngest son's measles, and whether it had been decided to put Tom into the corn-chandling trade. 'Much better let him be a farmer, Missis,' Sam would say, 'and marry a fat wife who can look after his money. For *he* won't, no more than I could, my dear.'

Robertson-Glasgow said that everyone loved Sammy, 'for the whole world's manliness and generosity seemed to have gathered into his heart.'

Sammy got on well with children. In some ways he never grew up himself. Jessop remembered him playing 'Bo Peep' with some grimy children in a tram; and there would sometimes be a bag of bullseyes in his pocket. Arthur Gilligan, captaining Sussex then, recalled on a visit to Burnham seeing Sammy walking through the streets with poor children taking it in turns to hold his hand.

According to Gilligan, Sammy used to go into the streets on Saturday mornings and ask the poorer children to go home and ask their mothers if they could come to breakfast with him on the morrow. Then, on Sunday morning, Sammy would entertain them to a splendid meal. But who prepared this breakfast, and where, he did not record.

Yet though Sammy had this easy rapport with children he did not know, as well as with women he met at dances and farmers' and shopkeepers' wives he chatted to, there does not seem to have been any real closeness in his relationships in either case. One or two who as sons of Somerset cricketers could be said to be more acquainted with Sammy than children on a tram or in the street remember this lack of intimacy. His godson, Nigel Daniell, remembers him as 'a rather forbidding figure'. Sammy was by nature closest to his fellow sportsmen and drinking companions, and happiest when swapping yarns and reminiscences with them.

In the mid-1920s Sammy spent quite a lot of time at Burnham; less, as time went on, for the golf and more for the bowls and the bar. Nigel Daniell, who was son of the Somerset captain, recalled how Sammy invited him, with another boy, to tea at Burnham Golf Club. Sammy left them in the room and tea was brought to the boys. But they did not see Sammy again until he reappeared as it was time to leave. He had, one may guess, been at the bar. Chatting for long to boys was not for him.

Another memory Nigel has of his godfather was receiving as a present one year a book, *The Story of a Red Deer*. The following year Sammy sent a book again: another copy of the same.

Robertson-Glasgow never saw Sammy bowling in his prime. He recalled him trundling a few down, in waistcoat and watch-chain, at the varsity nets when he was in his 50s. He gave Robertson-Glasgow valuable advice on bowling, and was always happy to help, whether it was a promising young cricketer or a county player who had a problem with his game.

Sammy also offered advice to young men on betting and drinking (advice he did not take himself). He told young ones to stick to beer and early hours. 'Whisky and one o'clock in the morning won't suit you, my dear,' he would say. As for backing horses: ''Tis a mug's game, and always will be,' he said, adding that he had backed the favourite to win the Derby, and was going up to see it run. 'No one like an old fool,' he said. 'But you young men needn't become old fools, nor young fools either. Still, I do love a race, if it is only between two cock sparrows across a road to get a bit of corn first.'

Reminiscences

'I have often been asked to write my reminiscences, and at last I am doing so.' Sammy was in his mid-50s when he sat down and penned some memories of his life on and off the field for *The Cricketer*. Later they appeared, largely the same, in a book, *My Reminiscences*, published by Chapman and Hall (1925), which also contained appreciations by Warner and Jessop. Surprisingly, the only illustration is not of Sammy the cricketer but a studio portrait of him in rugby shirt and shorts, seated and holding a rugby ball.

Sammy started off his book by saying there really should be two copies, one for his men pals and one for the general public; adding that 'many events have happened that I know of, especially in trips abroad, that would never do for the public to know.' If today's tabloid newspapers had been in existence then, we would have known, and Sammy would have doubtless featured in a good many sensational stories.

There is nothing in the book about the women in his life, if indeed there were any. Here was a sporting superstar, a magnificent specimen of a man, a bachelor with a freewheeling lifestyle, very popular with the ladies at social events. The groupies would have been after him today.

David Foot, in his history of Somerset cricket, *Sunshine, Sixes and Cider*, wrote that 'Sammy actually had a Victorian sportsman's asexuality. He was happiest in a bar, spinning yarns in interminable jest . . .' Peter Roebuck, in a chapter on Sammy, thought that he 'had a bit of fluff' in Taunton. He 'apparently had an accommodating lady in town, for ground-staff boys were under strict instructions not to disturb him on certain mornings.'

Sammy loved dancing, and in his reminiscences mentions the 'charming ladies' he met in Philadelphia, Boston, and Baltimore; and also going to a 'dancing salon' in Manchester after a match. The only woman he mentions by name is that 'ripping, sporting girl' called Brown on the voyage to Australia. According to MacBryan, when Sammy stopped to chat to Somerset farmers' wives, as he often did, their husbands 'did not object – they felt rather flattered.' But Sammy loved talking to anyone, anytime, and most probably these were entirely innocent occasions.

There is a hint that he may have had 'a reputation', even if undeserved. Robertson-Glasgow recalled a conversation with an elderly lady on a train. Talk turned to Sammy, and she told Robertson-Glasgow she had met him at a dance when she was 18. 'I had been told I must not dance with Sam,' she said – adding that she did! A different memory of Sammy from another lady: 'When I was a little girl, the impression I always had was that his breath smelt of whisky.'

Sam's published reminiscences, although not entirely about cricket and rugby, tell us little about his closest personal relationships. It is an aspect of his life about which it is unlikely we shall now learn more.

Nor shall we know (we can only speculate) whether, despite his host of friends and acquaintances and all the invitations, Sammy may not have increasingly suffered the darkness of loneliness as the years went on. Watching this or that sport, drinking and reminiscing and joking with his companions filled many of his days and evenings; but the time always came for a train or a walk through deserted streets back not to a wife or family but to an empty room in Taunton. Who can tell what feelings of loneliness may sometimes have descended on him there?

It may have been the need for a bit of money that made Sammy put some of his memories on paper. Jessop made a useful income from freelance journalism, and several other well-known cricketers of the day, such as Fry and MacLaren, wrote quite a lot, too. Had Sammy the ability to write as well as he could yarn, he could have been assured of a regular market. As it was he may have used a 'ghost' for the reminiscences, and not a very good 'ghost' at that; or perhaps a friendly local reporter took them down from dictation. Alas, they are not well composed, they are sometimes repetitive, and, although Sammy claimed 'a very retentive memory for the doings of years ago', not always accurate. Moreover they are tantalisingly brief on detail concerning some notable incidents, and omit altogether any reference to some of his most interesting matches and outstanding achievements.

Strangely for someone with a seemingly insatiable appetite for the game, Sammy said in his book that too much county cricket was being played. Certainly there were more championship matches than in recent times, but of course then there were no limited-over competitions. He felt that the Australians and South Africans were 'so much keener in the field' because they played less, and added: 'I once saw the Nottingham team in August at Taunton so tired that their dressing-room seemed more like an opium den than a changing room', with players having to be woken up when it was their time to bat.

This, he felt, was at least a cause of the deplorable fielding and catching he saw in county matches. He advocated more fielding practice, even during a match between batsmen departing and arriving, as the Australians and South Africans were already doing. 'To my mind there is nothing in cricket so delightful as to see a side field well', Sammy firmly believed.

He was supposed to have an aversion to sporting parsons, of whom there were several in county cricket. According to the writer, Sir Home Gordon, Sammy assured him one day 'with profound gravity' that their presence prevented the flow of genuine opinion, meaning uncensored language. Sammy recalled in his own book an occasion at Tonbridge when Somerset were playing Kent. Lionel Palairet had appendicitis and could not play, so he wired to Bedminster for the Rev. George Wood, who batted a few times for the county.

> He was playing very well and had got over 50 when he hit a ball into the country where another rev. gentleman was fielding, a splendid bat but the worst fielder in Europe, and never known to make a catch. He picked it up on the long hop and chucked it up, and the umpire gave my Christian out. Worst decision I ever saw! 'Christians awake!' said a man in the stand.

Still, his aversion to parsons on the cricket field did not extend to them all; his sometime host, Archie Wickham, was far from being his only clerical friend.

Sammy related one or two unusual or amusing incidents on the field:

> In a county match I hit a ball back very hard and hit the batsman at the other end on the arm and was caught by either mid-on or mid-off. I was playing for Wellington, Somerset v. the Incogs. there, and a Captain Greenway came in to bat and made 80 with huge hits and a bit of luck. Presently he hit a slow ball from me so high to square leg

that I sang out 'Mine', and went after it and caught it five yards from the pavilion. They had run three before I had done so.

In a club match at Wiveliscombe the other side went in and scored 40 for 8. Then:

Their captain came out and protested that the wicket was too short. He was mistaken, as it was 18 inches too long. Nevertheless, they started their innings again, and we had them out for 35. I expect we had been playing for years with the wicket too long. I remember I was hit on the head by a full pitch and had to retire first ball. 'What for?' I asked. 'L.b.w.' was the answer.

The reminiscences contain his assessment of many of his fellow players. The greatest all-rounders of his day, apart from Grace, were considered by Sammy to be Ted Arnold (Worcester), Len Braund (Somerset), Stanley Jackson (Yorkshire), and Gilbert Jessop (Gloucester).

Arnold, little remembered now outside the county he played for until ill-health brought his career to an end a little prematurely, scored a lot of runs, reaching 1,000 in ten seasons and taking 100 wickets in four of them. Sammy rated him 'at his best hard to beat as a medium-paced bowler'; but like Sammy he had only a few Test matches.

Braund, the man Surrey let go, is another all-rounder little remembered today outside his county, where for years he became the mainstay of the team. Sammy regarded him not only as the best all-rounder Somerset ever had, but as one of the greatest cricketers he knew. He was 'a fine bat, a splendid leg-break bowler, and a wonderful slip'. Braund 'spun off the pitch as quickly as a medium-paced bowler, and was as great a trier as ever I saw.' He was a magnificent fielder anywhere, though best remembered as a 'slipper'. He played in more than a score of Test matches, and some of his slip catches in these were quite exceptional.

Braund had given up playing about the time Sammy became county secretary and for many years served as an umpire. In later years he had both legs amputated, but still turned up at the Oval in a wheelchair.

Jackson, who succeeded Sammy as captain at Cambridge and later captained England, had an average of nearly 50 in his 33 Test innings, but it was as a bowler that Sammy particularly remembered him. They had shared the glory in the Gentlemen's remarkable win over the Players when the two of them bowled unchanged in each innings. Jackson, wrote Sammy, 'for several years was a much better bowler than he was given credit for. He had a lovely action and just over medium pace, with great command of the ball. He had a ball that just did three inches with his arm, mixed up with a good off-break.' And (something Sammy was always pleased to note) he 'showed up best when in a tight corner.'

But it was for Jessop that Sammy reserved his greatest praise – 'one of the most wonderful cricketers we have ever seen or are ever likely to see', and, playing for a weak county, a great match-winner. To class him just as a hitter, Sammy insisted, was absurd:

> No hitter pure and simple could get 50-odd centuries and double centuries in the time it took him to do. The wonderful thing about his batting was that he gave so few chances. Certainly at times he was out to deplorable strokes, but what batsman wouldn't be in trying to go the pace at 80 to 100 runs an hour?

The two had much in common in their approach to the game as players and captains; and both, too, were all-round sportsmen, Jessop excelling at almost as many games as Sammy.

Sammy recalled their first encounter, in 1894, at Taunton. Gloucester had nine wickets down for 60-odd when Jessop appeared. 'In less than 25 minutes he scored a wonderful innings of 60 not out. W.G. Grace asked my opinion of him. I said, "He has as good an eye as an eagle, and will get lots of runs".'

Jessop demoralised bowlers – they 'simply didn't know how to bowl at him,' said Sammy. '. . . off the same-length ball he would hit a six, a swish to leg for four, a beautiful back cut off the bails, or hit it past mid-off for four or six. Simply astonishing strokes!' He scored some fast double-centuries, breaking the record held by Sammy himself. His best knock, Sammy thought, was an innings at Hastings against the Players of the South, when he hit 191 in 90 minutes.

Jessop was more than a good enough fast bowler, too, to rate as a formidable all-rounder, but after his batting Sammy praised most his fielding – something he always liked to consider when assessing a player. He was simply 'the best cover point ever'. He reckoned that Jessop saved at the very least 30 runs in an innings. Sammy saw him on occasions swoop and throw so swiftly that when he hit the wicket the batsmen were only just crossing, providing the umpires with a problem in deciding who was out.

Among the great batsmen, Sammy remembered especially Abel, Ranji, Hobbs, and MacLaren. Of Abel, the diminutive Surrey professional known as 'The Guv'nor', he said:

> Standing only 5ft 5in, he withstood every sort of bowling (but that of Heseltine, of Hants) for years. They said at the time he could not play fast bowling. They said it, I didn't. Sometimes I got him out cheaply, but mostly he got lots of runs.

Sammy had occasion to remember: in 1899 Abel had hit 357 not out off the Somerset attack at the Oval. It is also true that the Surrey man did not do well against Heseltine, who dismissed him for ducks in three successive encounters.

After the 'Guv'nor', Surrey had the 'Master' – Jack Hobbs, who was beginning his career as Sammy's ended. He regretted that he did not see more of Hobbs' great innings, and remembered him (of course) not only for his 'so many lovely shots' but also for his fielding at cover, 'alert at all times'.

MacLaren was to be remembered most for that 424 he scored for Lancashire off the Somerset bowlers in 1895, but Sammy also recalled two of his several centuries on his happy hunting ground at Sydney. It was 'wonderful he way he played the ball'. He was 'a brilliant field . . . and I've never met a better judge of the game.'

One more batsman:

> A slim young Indian appeared at Cambridge in 1892 and began to get centuries galore on Parker's Piece for a town club. Someone discovered him and he got into the Cambridge XI. This young gentleman (known as 'Mr. Smith') was no other than the great cricketer Ranjitsinhji. He didn't do much for his Varsity in batting – still he made some wonderful catches in the slips. It was in 1895 whilst playing for Sussex that he created a sensation that has never been equalled since W.G. appeared at the Oval in Gents and Players as a boy of 17 [in fact, 16], ever so many years before. 'Mr. Smith' started his wonderful career at Lord's v. M.C.C. by getting 77 not out and 150.

Sammy forgot to add that on this remarkable debut Ranji also took six wickets.

Ranji, whose average for 500 first-class innings was 56, scored the highest of his 14 double centuries off Sammy and Co. at Taunton that day after a night of fishing. But Sammy rated as his best 200 the one he made on a sticky wicket against Middlesex when, facing Trott and Jack Hearne, then at their best, most batsmen (said Sammy) would have been glad to have got 30. 'He seemed to make up his mind as to what stroke he was going to play before the ball had got halfway up the pitch,' Sammy wrote. 'Like Jessop it was hard to know what to bowl to him as he had all the strokes on the board and then two more to go on with.'

Sammy thought that Sussex – against whom he himself had some of his best innings – were for a few years the best batting side in England. To open there were the great Fry and Joe Vine (described by Sammy as a hitter turned into a blocker), and they often scored 100 for the first wicket. Then there was Ranji; Sammy's fellow Australian, Murdoch; and one or two other talented batsmen to get rid of. He considered it a great pity that Fry could never go to Australia: 'the wickets there would have suited him to perfection.'

Like Jessop and others, Sammy regarded Kortright, of Essex, as the fastest bowler of all, though not the best. For that distinction he put first Surrey's Bill Lockwood, who, like Sammy, had at his command a splendid slow ball and was also a fine fielder and a good enough batsman to be regarded as an all-rounder.

Another Surrey professional no less admired was Lohmann:

> Just over medium pace, he varied his pace, break, and flight, and had a faster ball on any wicket, and especially deadly this one was on a bad wicket when he was turning them each way just enough to beat the bat. I would very much like to see these two-eyed stance batsmen perform against him. I think he would have half a dozen l.b.w. each innings . . . Unlike the present-day bowlers, sending three balls an over off the wicket, he wouldn't bowl 20 balls a day crooked, one had to play at nearly every ball.

'One of the most interesting fast bowlers' was the Lancashire amateur, Walter Brearley, among whose accomplishments was taking four Somerset wickets in four balls – two at the end of their first innings, then two more in his first two deliveries when they batted again. He took 17 wickets in all in this match at Old Trafford in 1905. Of Brearley, Sammy wrote:

> His great stamina stood him in good stead, as he could go on for hours without tiring. With a very short run he put every ounce into every ball. From the pavilion and from the ring every ball appeared alike, but not a bit of it, he had three distinct balls as well as a yorker. A look at his footholes easily showed this, but one can't see footholes from the batsman's end. One ball he delivered from near the stumps, the other from the extremest outside of the crease. Perhaps two were break-backs and one a swinger, and the other a straight one. His triumphs against Somerset were awful. I tried many times to knock him off when he was skittling my side out. But it was ever the same sad tale, home to the hutch you go.

Sammy thought that when he had lost his bowling a bit, Brearley should have gone in for batting. A little practice and, he felt, he would have made a good bat.

> But he was always so keen to get at 'em with the ball. A wonderful fellow to see come in last, hardly ever took the trouble to come out through the gate, generally jumped over the rails or over somebody's shoulder, nearly ran to the wicket, and if he was out first ball would remark to the bowler, 'Well bowled, that was a good 'un'.

But if Brearley ranked as one of the most interesting bowlers, it was Spofforth, the Demon from New South Wales, who Sammy described as '*the* most interesting' of all those he ever saw. He got his name, as Sammy supposed, from the time when he and Harry Boyle dismissed the M.C.C. for 19 in 1878. Sammy did not think Boyle had quite his share of the credit for this, as he got nearly as many wickets and in addition took two or three good catches off Spofforth at forward short leg. Sammy wrote:

> Spofforth was acclaimed a fast bowler; he was medium-fast with a fast yorker, and had more guile than any bowler I ever saw. He had a perfect follow through, and he delivered every ball with the same action, and as he looked all legs,

arms, and nose, it was very hard to distinguish what ball was coming along next.

The *best* medium-fast bowler, however, was in Sammy's view Jack Hearne, the greatest of three brother professionals:

> What a trier. He at times was the only professional on the Middlesex side. He never seemed to get sunburnt, and was generally known as the 'white slave'. It would have been much better to have called him the 'white man' for a better fellow never stepped on to the cricket field . . . He could bowl all day, and generally had to do so on good wickets.

Among the other bowlers Sammy singled out was one from Somerset: 'Farmer' Jack White, still today ranked as one of the great slow left-armers. He used to go straight from working on his farm near the Quantocks to bowl for long spells at Taunton. He had been coached at school by Tyler. White would bowl all day if necessary, and Sammy wrote:

> He has got quite used to having catches missed off him; well for him he has, otherwise his fair hair would now be snow white. He gets his 150 wickets yearly, no matter what the wickets are like. Being a good bat and field and a cheery soul, no wonder he is the idol of the Somerset crowds no matter where he goes. In bowling he relies on length and flight. For the first month or two each year he spins the ball well, but he has so much bowling he loses this a bit in August.

White's greatest triumph was in the 1928–29 Tests in Australia. At Adelaide in great heat he bowled 124 overs and 5 balls and took 13 wickets for 256. When he returned to Taunton, Sammy was there at the railway station to meet him along with the Mayor and local M.P., and a civic procession made its way through the streets of the county town.

But the man Sammy ranked as the greatest left-arm bowler was Kent's Colin Blythe, who had taken over 2,500 first-class wickets when he went away to war, to be killed near Passchendaele in 1917. Not only did Sammy think him the best (and 'a charming personality', loved by his team-mates), but also the most interesting to study:

That leisurely run up to the wicket, just the same all day long (he seldom had to field all day long), a slow swing of the arm, it all looked so simple until one had to play him. On several occasions I got runs against him, and once or twice a 100. Still, I was always looking out for a ball on the blind spot, then I seemed to lose it somewhere. It generally meant my hearing the death rattle. I fancy he thought of every ball he bowled and very often puzzled his wicketkeeper as much as he did the batsman.

Sammy devoted a short chapter in his reminiscences to 'Some "Lobsters"', the bowlers who lobbed the ball – although he preferred as an explanation of how they got their name 'the crab-like walk that they marched to the wicket'. Sammy himself took a good many wickets in club cricket, including all ten in an innings once, with his underarm deliveries, and there were a surprising number of 'lobsters' still in the first-class game even less than a century ago.

Far and away the best lob bowler he ever saw or played against, wrote Sammy, was the Sussex professional, Walter Humphreys. Sammy was one of those who got the better of him, but, he declared:

I would sooner have played against anyone else on the side. He was, in my opinion, as difficult to deal with as any of the googly merchants I have ever seen since. He had his right-hand sleeve flapping (lots of complaints about it, but without avail), and I came across very few people who could tell which way the ball was going to break.

One season Humphreys took 150 wickets with his lobs, and Sammy remembered seeing him achieve a hat-trick against the Australians at Brighton in the 1880s, his second on the same ground against the tourists.

One of Sammy's anecdotes concerns a very young Jack Sharp, later to captain Lancashire and to play both cricket and soccer for England.

I was playing for the M.C.C. at Hereford. I was having a practice with a post behind me as a stump. A boy of about 14 bowled to me and was as keen as could be, and hit the post once or twice. We were one short, so I suggested playing the boy. We did, and I may say we were in a bad way when the boy joined me. I got 60 odd, and the boy about 15 not out.

Sammy gave the youngster his bat, with his initials, S.M.J.W., on the back. That was in the early 1890s. Some years later, when Somerset were playing Lancashire at Bath, one of the visiting team came and introduced himself. It was Sharp, and he still had the bat and used it in that match.

The most powerful hitters Sammy remembered were Charles Thornton and George Bonnor. In practice at Brighton, Thornton hit a ball 168 yards and in a match at Canterbury 152 yards. In Sammy's Cambridge days Thornton, who captained visiting teams several times, hit Sammy out of Fenner's twice.

Bonnor, from New South Wales, also made Sammy suffer, and which was the greater hitter was often discussed among cricketers. Sammy regarded Bonnor as 'simply a slogger'. He was a giant of a man, 6ft 5in. tall, and after he had taken two splendid slip catches with his long arms someone asked him where he practised his fielding. 'I just go down to the river' (Sammy thought it was the Yarra Yarra) 'and catch the swallows as they flit by.'

Two players Sammy thought people might be surprised to find in his list of notable hitters were Grace and Lionel Palairet. The former was 'so powerful and never looked as if he was hitting'; and the Somerset man was 'so graceful and looked to be playing only forward'.

Among wicket-keepers Sammy saw two of the greats, Alfred Lyttleton and Dick Pilling, only a few times, and recalled that 'they were both very neat and stood up to the fastest of bowling, and made as little fuss as if it was medium-pace.'

The man Sammy thought of as 'the best everyday wicket-keeper' – not the most brilliant, but the most consistent – was Arthur Newton, who had given Sammy a wicket with his first ball for Somerset with a superb leg-side stumping. At the time Sammy was writing in the 1920s A.E., as he was known, was keeping wicket sometimes for Somerset Stragglers, although in his 70s (he stumped five in an innings around this time, after having cycled to the match). He was still playing in his early 80s.

Mordecai Sherwin, of Nottingham, was 'the largest wicket-keeper I ever saw – he must have weighed 16 or 17 stone, and yet for many years was as active as a cat.' Sammy recalled him declaring when a bowler had appealed for l.b.w. or a catch at the wicket, 'That wasn't out' before the umpire had replied 'Not out'.

There was another Somerset keeper who stood up to the fastest of bowling and who Sammy reckoned should have played for England. As it was, Lilley was then in his prime and so Henry Martyn, a tall and long-armed man, had to make do with a few matches for the Gentlemen against the Players in the early years of this century.

Once Sammy saw him have some teeth nearly knocked out by a delivery from a fast bowler, George Gill. Sammy the first-aider was quickly in action. He told Martyn 'Hold your head still', and then: 'I shoved them back into their sockets. They are still there, although a bit discoloured. A dentist wanted to take them out. I said, "Nonsense, they will grow", and they did. He went on keeping as if nothing had happened.'

There could, of course, be no mention of wicketkeepers without recalling his old room-mate at Cambridge, MacGregor – 'a great judge of the game and the best captain I ever saw.' MacGregor 'looked rather bored' when keeping wicket, but, said Sammy, 'if one thought so and lifted one's toe for the fraction of a second one was soon disillusioned and had one's marching orders at once.'

Sammy believed that two of the great bowlers of the day would never have been the success they were but for MacGregor. They were Australians, Trott and Frank Tarrant, both from Victoria and playing for Middlesex under MacGregor's captaincy. He thought it was MacGregor who made Tarrant bowl slower. 'When first I played with Tarrant down in Wales he bowled nothing but fast stuff. When next I saw him under MacGregor he was a bowler, and finished his career in being one of the best all-round cricketers in the world.' There were many others who shared this assessment of Tarrant (who in eight seasons did the double), but like Sammy he was handicapped when it came to being chosen for Test matches by being an Australian in England. In fact he did not even get the handful of Test matches that Sammy did.

Grace was playing his first game for the Gentlemen before Sammy was born, and so he never had to face the great man's medium-paced bowling. By Sammy's time he was 'slow and very accurate', continually pegging away at the leg stump or thereabouts, with a trap at long square leg. 'I got a century and lots of fifties against him, but I was never comfortable,' Sammy said. There were not so many wickets now for Grace, but still plenty of runs: Sammy had good cause to remember his 100th hundred off the Somerset bowling at the age of 47, and he hit another 26 centuries before he hung up his bat.

The paths of the two crossed many times, as has already been seen, and they went beagling together often. The hounds seemed to take more notice of Grace than of the master, Sammy thought. Even approaching 60 W.G.'s stamina was extraordinary: 'he was always merry and bright from Monday morning until Saturday night,' – as Sammy, who caroused with him on quite a few occasions, knew from experience.

One of Sammy's very earliest meetings with Grace was in 1888, the year after Queen Victoria's Jubilee, while Sammy was still in his first year at Cambridge. The two were playing in the Scarborough Festival at the end of the season. After a match they went to a theatre and then on to a dance given by the 'Jubilee Plunger'. This was Ernest Benzon, a wealthy young man who squandered a fortune on the horses at this time. At supper at the dance, Grace and Sammy took in, arm in arm, the little 'drummer boy' (in fact a girl of about 4ft 6in). 'How people laughed,' Sammy recalled, 'and how the dear old man chuckled over it.' Of Benzon, who lost in a short time more money than Sammy saw in his life, Sammy remarked: 'What a fool the "J.P." was! But aren't most of us the same?'

Although in his reminiscences Sammy referred to Grace as 'an artful toad', he would, according to Robertson-Glasgow, hear nothing against his old friend from others.

W.G.'s older brother, Dr. E.M. Grace, was no less admired by Sammy, who was astounded at the number of wickets he took with his lobs in club cricket in his later years – 200 or even 300 in a season. E.M. also liked to keep on bowling, whatever the batsmen were doing. Sammy recalled that in one match in his own early days he was hitting the ball about a lot and someone suggested to E.M. that he had a change of bowling. His reply was: 'Very well, I think it would be a good thing. I will change ends.' As he did.

Another story Sammy told was of how, in Somerset's early days as a first-class county, E.M. hit 70 or so for Gloucester off the bowling while Sammy was still sending them down very fast. This was despite the batsman being handicapped with a dreadful thumb, matter oozing from under the nail. Sammy went on:

> He bent down very much in those days and I hit him on the bad thumb twice. Someone in the crowd called out, 'Why don't you hold an inquest on him', for E.M. was Coroner

for West Gloucester. E.M. said to Hewett [then Somerset captain], 'I can't stand this', and toddled off to where the voice came from. The man who had made the remark said to a boy near him, 'The doctor is after you,' and the boy ran away.

Sammy regarded E.M. Grace, even when he was over 50, as easily the best point he ever saw. Even if a hitter were in he would stand within eight yards of the bat. Stoddart told Sammy that in his first encounter, E.M. 'took the ball off his bat.'

His bravery as a fielder was one of several things he had in common with Sammy, though their styles in both batting and bowling were different. They were both cheery men, 'the life and soul of the game wherever he played', Sammy said of E.M. and could have said of himself. They were both great tellers of stories. 'At luncheon he was full of good tales – and bad ones' said Sammy. But unlike Sammy E.M. could never be persuaded to write his reminiscences.

The Last Days

In his later years Sammy suffered a good deal of pain from rheumatism, about which he would joke. But as a new decade dawned, he could not but be aware of something more sinister, about which he could not joke: a growth in his gullet.

He made an appointment early in the year of 1931 to see a specialist in London's Harley Street. On his way he called on an old cricketing friend, John Poynton, himself a Harley Street man of note. The two had played together for Somerset back in the early 1890s.

Poynton now saw 'a broken man', and soon afterwards the consultant Sammy visited confirmed that his condition was 'inoperable and fatal'. His death certificate was to show that he had cancer of the oesophagus, a type of cancer often associated with excessive alcohol.

It was now April, a few days after his 64th birthday. He made a last journey from Taunton to Bridgwater, where he went to a club of which he had long been a member and had a lengthy chat with an old friend, Colonel E. Trevor. The following day, back in Taunton, he went into the Ventura Nursing Home and underwent an operation. That week the local newspapers gave the news to shocked readers that although the operation 'for internal trouble' was 'successful', his condition gave rise to grave anxiety.

Then the April 18 issue of the *County Gazette* gave false hope of better news. Sammy was in less pain and was receiving visitors. One of these was a reporter from the newspaper, to whom Sammy gave the last of his many interviews. The *Gazette* man wrote:

> He is keenly interested in the forthcoming cricket season and ... quite agreed with the proposal put forward by Somerset C.C., though rejected by the M.C.C., that in the interests of the less prosperous counties fewer matches should be played.
>
> 'There is too much county cricket,' he emphasised, 'especially when a touring side is visiting this country ... It is not generally known that the Australians do not play for

three days before any Test match, whereas our men come
from all parts of England, hurriedly leaving county games to
under-take probably long journeys.'

A week later the same newspaper reported that Sammy was that
day leaving the nursing home for a private residence. 'He has made
progress, his many friends will be glad to hear, but will still require
careful nursing,' it said.

The truth was that he had been taken there to die. Early in the
morning of April 30, at Melville House, Middle Street, two or three
six hits away from the county ground, his pain was over. A few more
hours later the first Somerset trial match of the season began with the
flag flying at half mast, and at the Oval, where a trial was also in
progress, the flag there was also lowered.

Sammy Woods had never had his own home, and it was fitting that
he was to spend his last days in one of the many homes of others in
which he had over the years always been a welcome visitor or guest.
In this case Melville House, a substantial building now housing legal
chambers and other offices, had been for some time the home of a
prominent local solicitor, Colonel O.R.M. Channer, a member of the
county cricket club and a friend.

Not only did Sammy never have a home of his own; he left little
in the way of material possessions. In his last years he must have had
the use of the sum of £1,250 which had been invested by trustees of
his benefit fund in 1907, for his entire assets in England were valued
for probate at £137. There were presumably further assets in
Australia, for the following year in Sydney a figure of £A641 was
assessed.

He left 'some Japanese bonds' to his Bridgwater friend Humphrey
Burrington; and his gold watch, chain and sleeve links to E.S.
Massey Poyntz. The former had a few games for Somerset, the latter
played over 100 and also captained the county in 1913–14. The rest
of his small estate went to the sister, Amy Dean, who was living in
Exmouth.

But if he had little to leave in the material sense, he left many
memories, and to his friends his death was very much a personal loss.
His Harley Street friend, Poynton, penned a few deeply-felt lines:

For those of my time with his death our cricket died, for we
had known him in his prime, a superb athlete, a most

154

lovable cheery man, with a kind heart, a nice singing voice,
a teller of good tales, and never beat . . . the life and soul of
us all, of cricketers and of crowds who watched him.

And, after a few lines about his cricket, the final words:

No 'swagger', just a big man child.

Thousands of words were written about him in the obituaries. *The
Times* said that among University athletes few names would stand
higher. The *News Chronicle* said he was 'not only a magnificent rugby
footballer and a dashing all-round cricketer; but he was one of those
commanding figures who inevitably takes the leadership in manly
exercises.' *The Cricketer*, in a long account headed 'A King of Cricket',
said that his keenness was such that he never abandoned hope while a
ball remained to be bowled and that 'His title of "Greatheart" was
well deserved.'

A leading Westcountry newspaper, the *Bristol Times and Mirror*,
inevitably coupled his name with that of W.G. Grace, different in
temperament and style, but both big-hearted men who devoted
themselves to cricket and did so much for their respective counties.
And the writer went on to say: 'Popularity never spoilt him. Until the
end he remained a generous-hearted boy. Indeed he may be described
as the Peter Pan of cricket, for he never quite grew up.'

And in the columns devoted to his career in the *Somerset County
Gazette*, one line stands out: '. . . a bonnie fighter who made his
keenness contagious.'

A few days after his death there appeared in *The Times* a tribute by
'Joseph', which hid the identity of a former county player who had
appeared under both 'The Colonel' and Sammy. He wrote:

> . . . Hewett is gone, and now 'Sammy' is gone, and I venture
> to believe that there is not a heart that knew him which does
> not beat sadly at those words. The remembrance of him in
> his prime is the vision of a magnificent man. He may not
> have been 'clever' or 'erudite', but he combined the courage
> of the heroes of old Homer with physical strength and
> kindliness, and to those was joined the simplicity of a child.
>
> That great and unusual courage possessed by him was
> never better shown than at the Oval in the palmy days of
> Richardson and Lockwood, when with four of our side out

for 20 runs he would come in, hit those bowlers all over the ground, and make us smaller men take heart once more. What a mid-off to Tyler's slow left-arm bowling! Only those who fielded with him can realise what he caught, what he stopped, and the ground he covered. His bowling when at its best was superb. Never tired and never beaten, ever happy and care-free, to have played with 'Sammy' in his golden prime is to have lived happy days, and to have learnt the real meaning of courage, strength, and cheerfulness. To know that he is no longer in suffering and distress is to see in a tear-dimmed picture Lord's, the glorious sun, and 'Sammy' at the Pavilion gate, cheered to the echo by a happy welcoming Bank Holiday crowd.

It rained on the day of the funeral, Monday, May 4, but crowds of townsfolk turned out to join his friends and sporting companions in mourning his passing. At Lord's now the flag was flown at half-mast. The coffin had been taken overnight to St John's church, where the vicar was the Rev. F.E. Spurway, who occasionally kept wicket for Somerset through the 1920s. It laid there in the sanctuary between glowing candles.

Mourners started arriving nearly an hour before the service began, and soon there was no room for everyone in the church. Helping Mr Spurway conduct the service were another clerical wicketkeeper, Sammy's old friend 'The Bishop', Archie Wickham, and the Rev. P.T. Pryce-Michell, a friend since his Cambridge days.

Those at the service and the interment in St Mary's cemetery, about a mile from the town centre, came from far afield. There were representatives of the M.C.C. and the England Rugby Union, county cricketers, and many other sportsmen. Among the wreaths piled high in the hearse and a following coach were the red and white roses of Lancashire and Yorkshire. The long list of mourners in the local Press included a bishop, an admiral, and a couple of generals, and there were many humbler folk. Village cricket clubs sent their representatives. The ordinary folk of Taunton lined the route. The headline in one local paper summed it up: 'A Town in Mourning'.

The rain still fell as the plain oak coffin was slowly lowered into a grave lined with narcissi and evergreens.

Later a solid stone monument was erected at the grave, sited only a few yards from the main road linking Taunton and Wellington. It was provided by the Somerset County Cricket and Rugby Clubs, and bears the simple inscription:

S.M.J. Woods
1867–1931
A Tribute to
a Great Sportsman

Through the trees can be seen the Quantocks, the green hills of Somerset which Sammy Woods, the much-travelled sportsman from Sydney, New South Wales, said he loved more than anywhere else in the world.

INDEX